WHAT'S COOKING
Mediterranean

Anne White

THUNDER BAY
P·R·E·S·S

San Diego, California

THUNDER BAY
P · R · E · S · S

Thunder Bay Press
An imprint of the Advantage Publishers Group
5880 Oberlin Drive, San Diego, CA 92121-4794
www.advantagebooksonline.com

A Parragon book, Parragon, Queen Street House, 4 Queen Street, Bath BA1 1HE, UK

Library of Congress Cataloging-in-Publication Data

White, Anne
    What's cooking. Mediterranean / Anne White.–North American ed.
        p. cm.
    title: Mediterranean
    Includes index.
    ISBN 1-57145-255-9
        1. Cookery, Mediterranean. I. Title

TX725.M35 W49 2000
641.59′92–dc21

                                                            00-027321

Printed in China
3 4 5 6 7 06 05 04 03 02
Produced by Haldane Mason, London

Acknowledgments
Editorial Consultant: Felicity Jackson
Photography: Colin Bowling, Paul Forrester, and Stephen Brayne
Home Economists and Stylist: David Morgan, Vicki Smallwood, Gina Steer
All props supplied by Barbara Stewart at Surfaces.

NOTE

Unless otherwise stated, milk is assumed to be full fat,
eggs are medium, and pepper is freshly ground black pepper.

Recipes using uncooked eggs should be
avoided by infants, the elderly, pregnat women, and anyone
suffering from an illness

Contents

Introduction

Anyone who has spent even the briefest amount of time along the Mediterranean can not have come away without a lasting recollection of the wonderful aromas and flavors of the region. "Robust" and "intense" are just two of the appropriate adjectives to describe the range of dishes you find from coastal Spain through France, Italy, Greece, and Turkey and along North Africa.

Most of the region's best-known dishes are, in essence, simple fare produced for generations from plentiful home-grown or local ingredients. Although far from the sparkling blue waters of the Mediterranean, we are now lucky enough to have a wide range of these ingredients in our local stores. However, to capture the true sun-kissed flavors of the region, it is important to seek out the best-quality produce. All the recipes in this book are simple and easy to prepare, but because most are so simple, they rely on ripe, flavor-filled ingredients for their character.

OLIVE OIL

As you sample food from the different countries along the Mediterranean, you will soon appreciate that they share many ingredients, with olive oil probably being the most common. And what a variety of olive oils there are to choose from—you will find them ranging in color from almost emerald green to the palest yellow, with flavors that range from peppery and spicy to very mild. There are even olive oils with a hint of chocolate.

If you are used to cooking with other vegetable oils, such as sunflower or corn, olive oil can be an acquired taste, and the only way to find the oils you like the most is to taste many. The best place to do this is usually in small delicatessens specializing in Mediterranean produce, where free tastings are more likely to occur than at supermarkets.

You'll also find olive oils available in different grades. Extra-virgin is produced from the first pressing, so it has the fullest flavor and, consequently, is the most expensive. Save this to use in salad dressings and with uncooked ingredients, where heat doesn't diminish the flavor. For cooking, choose an oil simply labeled as "olive oil."

Much is made of the healthy qualities of the Mediterranean diet, because olive oil contains so little saturated fat, the type of fat possibly linked to heart disease. But remember, it is still a fat, so it should be used sparingly.

TOMATOES

Sun-ripened, juicy tomatoes are synonymous with Mediterranean food, giving flavor to both cooked and uncooked dishes. When you can only buy flavorless hot-house tomatoes, a good-quality canned variety is a better option for cooked dishes.

Italian plum tomatoes are a good choice for most Mediterranean dishes, but the larger tomatoes and small cherry tomatoes are also ideal for many recipes. When you are buying tomatoes, look for smooth, undamaged skins and textures that feel just soft when you squeeze lightly.

Try preserving flavorful tomatoes in Oven-dried Tomatoes (see page 174) to use in the colder months. When you have a large quantity of tomatoes lacking in flavor, use them for recipes such as Slow-cooked Tomato Sauce (see page 192) or Ratatouille (see page 134), both of which freeze well and have other ingredients that compensate for the weak tomato flavor.

GARLIC

Garlic is the all-important flavoring in many Mediterranean dishes, and it is also used both cooked and uncooked. Raw it can be too strong for some, but when cooked slowly its flavor softens and whole cloves become meltingly soft and deliciously sweet.

Do not buy garlic bulbs that have sprouted because that is a sign they are old and may taste bitter. The best garlic has compact cloves and tight-fitting skin. Don't store it in the refrigerator—it keeps best at room temperature in a dark location, which is why many people use garlic pots with small holes so air can circulate.

Roasted Garlic Delicious smeared on broiled chicken pieces or steaks, or on toasted bread. Put a whole bulb of unpeeled garlic in a piece of foil, large enough to enclose it, and drizzle with olive oil. Roast in a preheated oven at 375°F for 40 minutes, or until the cloves are very soft when pierced with a knife. Unwrap the bundle and squeeze the cloves out of their papery skins.

EGGPLANTS

Elongated eggplants, with their deep-purple, smooth skins, also symbolize Mediterranean cooking to many people—they are an essential ingredient to the French and Italians.

You will find most recipes specify to sprinkle cut pieces of eggplant with salt and leave the pieces to stand for about 30 minutes before using. This simple technique draws out moisture to prevent the flesh from becoming soggy and helps to eliminate bitterness, which is a characteristic of older eggplants. After they have drained, be sure to rinse them well to remove the excess salt. If the eggplant slices are going to be baked or fried, pat them dry with paper towels first.

At the height of summer, Mediterranean market stalls are piled high with miniature varieties of eggplants with pale purple or almost-white skins. Local chefs use these to make attractive appetizers or edible garnishes. Only buy eggplants that feel smooth and firm. Size doesn't affect the flavor, but remember that the thicker an eggplant is, the more seeds it is likely to contain.

Eggplants have a natural affinity with tomatoes, so you'll often find the two ingredients combined.

SEAFOOD

With the teeming waters of the Mediterranean, it is not surprising fish and shellfish feature regularly in the local diets. Bouillabaisse, the classic French seafood stew that is a feast in a bowl, is an example of the wonderful use made of the daily catches. But, even at Mediterranean restaurants, the dish is an expensive feast, so instead enjoy the flavor with the scaled-down version of Seafood Stew (see page 100), or Mediterranean Fish Soup (see page 98).

Whether you are buying fresh fish or shellfish, the golden rule is the same—only buy the freshest available and cook it on the same day. Fresh fish should have clear, shiny eyes and red gills. When you pick up a whole fish, it should be firm, not floppy. If it droops, it has been out of the water for more than a day and should be left on the fish counter.

Cut pieces of fish, such as swordfish or tuna steaks, should have a clear, clean looking surface. White fish, such as a sea bass, should have a pearl-like color.

Fish should not smell "fishy." Instead, it should have a fresh, almost sweet aroma, as if it has come out of the water only a few hours before.

Remember that shellfish, such as mussels, oysters, and clams, should actually be alive when you buy them. You can tell they are fresh if their shells are closed. Shrimp, on the other hand, are usually frozen before they are shipped.

As a general rule, the less time you cook seafood the better the flavor and texture will be.

FRESH HERBS

As you drive along the Mediterranean coast at the height of summer, the air is scented with rosemary, basil, cilantro, dill, oregano, sage, flat-leaf parsley, and thyme growing in profusion. Winter stews and casseroles use dried herbs, but only the freshest, fullest-flavored herbs will do for the summer dishes and salads. The obvious solution if you plan to do a lot of Mediterranean cooking is to grow your own, so you always have a supply. Even a single pot of various herbs growing on your window sill will make a difference to your cooking.

When you are buying fresh herbs, reject any that do not look fresh and vibrant; limp, dull-looking herbs without their full aroma will not add anything to your dish. Be sure to sniff the herbs before you buy, because greenhouse-grown ones can look fantastic but lack the essential flavor.

Basil Where would Italian cooks be without this zingy-tasting and fragrant herb? It has an affinity with tomatoes and is often included in pasta dishes and soups. It is difficult to preserve successfully, so if you have too much, freeze large quantities of Pesto Sauce (see page 124) or Pistou sauce (see page 28). Do not freeze the leaves because they will turn black and loose their aroma. Instead, layer the leaves with sea salt in a non-metallic, tightly covered container and leave for up to 3 months. The leaves can then be added to cooked dishes.

Cilantro Also popular in Asian cooking, this herb has a distinctive taste that not everyone is familiar with. It is used in many Turkish, Moroccan, and Greek recipes. Be careful when you are buying because it looks similar to flat-leaf parsley and often the only way to tell them apart is to taste a leaf. Use in soups and with seafood recipes and pickles.

Dill This feathery green herb with its distinctive flavor goes well with all seafood and tomato dishes, and it particularly used in Greek cooking.

Parsley Mediterranean cooks favor the flat-leaf variety of this all-purpose herb, sometimes referred to as Italian parsley. Use generously in salads and as a garnish. Always use fresh or frozen, and avoid dried.

Marjoram The Greeks consider this the "joy of the mountains" and it features in the islands' cuisines. It is good with pork and poultry dishes.

Oregano Also known as wild marjoram, this is a pungent herb that should be used sparingly. It dries well, making a good addition to winter casseroles and pizza toppings. Try it with tomato, zucchini and eggplant dishes.

Rosemary Strongly flavored, this shrub herb should be very young if using in uncooked dishes. It's a natural partner to lamb. Throw branches on barbecue coals to add an authentic aroma, or use twigs as skewers.

Sage Popular both fresh and dried in Italian cooking, sage has a pronounced flavor and a little goes a long way. Good for boiling with beans and for flavoring broiled poultry, the purple-leafed variety also makes an attractive garnish.

Thyme The small leaves are good for flavoring tomatoes, stews, and grilled meats. It also goes well with olives.

Herbes de Provence When you have an abundance of summer herbs, use them to make this classic French combination of herbs and spices. You need to dry the herbs first, then put equal amounts of fennel seed, lavender flowers, marjoram, rosemary, sage, summer savory, and thyme into an airtight container and store for up to 6 months. Herbes de Provence is traditionally used to flavor cooked poultry, meat, and vegetable dishes, especially during the winter. It is also good in cooked pasta sauces and pizza toppings.

Snacks & Appetizers

One of the most enjoyable aspects of Mediterranean cuisines is the emphasis on snacks and simple dishes that are served at almost any time of the day. The Spanish, for example, are renowned for their tapas, and the Greeks, Turks, and Moroccans enjoy nothing more than sitting down at a table filled with a selection of appetizers, called meze.

The recipes in this chapter are easy to prepare and always popular because they are so flavorful. They are also the type of food to enjoy at relaxed, social occasions, and recipes such as Hummus, Taramasalata, Tapenade, Eggplant Spread, and Aioli, instantly capture the atmosphere of easy-going, sunny Mediterranean meals.

When it's a hot day and you don't want to spend time in a steaming kitchen, where better to look for inspiration than the Mediterranean? For no-cook recipes, try the Gazpacho, Garlic & Almond Soup, or Ceviche, along with any of the mouthwatering dips listed above. And what can possibly beat prosciutto with melon and figs on a hot day? If you want a sophisticated start for a meal, but again don't want to cook, try Crab & Celery Root Remoulade. Serve it with a chilled bottle of Provençal rosé and your dinner will be off to a fantastic start.

Hummus

Quick and easy to make, this dip features regularly on Mediterranean menus.
Serve it with fingers of pita bread or vegetable sticks for dipping.

Makes about a scant 3 cups

INGREDIENTS

7 oz. dried chickpeas
2 large garlic cloves
7 tbsp. extra-virgin olive oil
2¹/₂ tbsp. tahini

1 tbsp. lemon juice, or to taste
salt and pepper

TO GARNISH:
extra-virgin olive oil
paprika
fresh cilantro

1 Place the chickpeas in a large bowl. Pour in at least twice the volume of cold water to chickpeas and let stand for at least 12 hours until they double in size.

2 Drain the chickpeas. Put them in a large flameproof casserole or saucepan and add twice the volume of water to the chickpeas. Bring to a boil and boil hard for 10 minutes, skimming the surface.

3 Lower the heat and let simmer for 1 hour, skimming the surface if necessary, or until the chickpeas are tender. Meanwhile, cut the garlic cloves in half, remove the pale green or white cores and coarsely chop. Set aside.

4 Drain the chickpeas, reserving 4 tablespoons of the cooking liquid. Put the olive oil, garlic, tahini, and lemon juice in a food processor and blend until a smooth paste forms.

5 Add the chickpeas and pulse until they are finely ground but the hummus is still lightly textured. Add a little of the reserved cooking liquid if the mixture is too thick. Season with salt and pepper to taste.

6 Transfer to a bowl, cover with plastic wrap, and chill until ready to serve. To serve, drizzle with some olive oil, sprinkle a little paprika over, and garnish with fresh cilantro.

Taramasalata with Pita Wedges

Forget the artificially dyed, bright pink taramasalata sold in tourist restaurants or many supermarkets. This is the version you will find in Greek homes.

Makes about 2 cups

INGREDIENTS

8 oz. smoked cod's roe
1 small onion, finely chopped
1 garlic clove
2 oz. fresh white bread without crusts
finely grated rind of 1 lemon

4 tbsp. lemon juice, plus extra to taste, if desired
$^2/_3$ cup extra-virgin olive oil
6 tbsp. hot water
salt and pepper

hollowed-out tomatoes, to serve
fresh flat-leaf parsley sprigs, to garnish

PITA WEDGES:
2 pita breads
olive oil, for brushing

1 Remove the skin from the smoked cod's roe. Put the roe and onion in a food processor and process until well blended and smooth. Add the garlic and process again.

2 Break the bread into the food processor, then add the lemon rind and 4 tablespoons of the lemon juice. Process again until the bread is well incorporated.

3 With the motor running, gradually add the olive oil

through the feed tube, as if making a mayonnaise. When all the oil is incorporated, add the hot water and process again. Add salt and pepper to taste, plus extra lemon juice if desired. Spoon into a bowl, cover with plastic wrap and chill until ready to serve.

4 To make the pita wedges, using a serrated knife, cut the pita breads in half through the center. Cut each half into 6–8 wedges, depending on the size. Place on a cookie sheet and brush

the inside surfaces of the wedges with olive oil.

5 Bake in a preheated oven at 350°F for 20 minutes. Place on wire racks to cool.

6 Spoon the taramasalata into the tomato shells, garnish with parsley, and serve with the pita wedges for dipping.

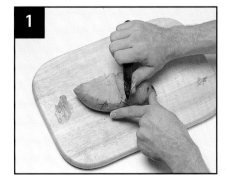

Tzatziki

No collection of Mediterranean recipes would be complete without this creamy Greek dip. Simple to make, it is very refreshing on a hot day and is particularly good for parties.

Makes about 3⅓ cups

INGREDIENTS

2 large cucumbers
2½ cups Greek Strained Yogurt
(see page 182), or natural
thick yogurt

3 garlic cloves, crushed
1 tbsp. finely chopped fresh dill
1 tbsp. extra-virgin olive oil
salt and pepper

TO SERVE:
1 tbsp. sesame seeds
cayenne pepper
fresh dill sprigs (optional)

1 Using the coarse side of a grater, grate the cucumbers into a bowl lined with an absorbent, perforated kitchen cloth. Pull up the corners of the cloth to make a tight bundle and squeeze very hard to extract all the moisture (see Cook's Tip).

2 Put the cucumbers in a bowl and stir in the yogurt, garlic, dill, olive oil, and salt and pepper to taste. Cover with plastic wrap and chill for at least 3 hours for the flavors to blend.

3 When ready to serve, remove the dip from the refrigerator and stir. Taste and adjust the seasoning if necessary.

4 Put the sesame seeds in a small, ungreased skillet and dry-fry them over medium heat until they turn golden and start to give off their aroma. Immediately pour them out of the pan onto the tzatziki—they will sizzle.

5 Lightly dip the tip of a dry pastry brush into some cayenne pepper. Tap a light sprinkling of cayenne all over the tzatziki. Garnish with fresh dill, if desired, and serve.

COOK'S TIP

It is essential to squeeze all the moisture out of the cucumbers in Step 1, or the dip will be watery and separate.

COOK'S TIP

The ungarnished Tzatziki will keep, covered, for up to 3 days in the refrigerator.

Eggplant Spread

This simple, quick dip is so good that it is often called "poor man's caviar." It is probably Middle Eastern in origin, but is found on many menus throughout the Mediterranean, especially in Greek tavernas.

Makes about 1¾ cups

INGREDIENTS

2 large eggplants
1 tomato
1 garlic clove, chopped
4 tbsp. extra-virgin olive oil
2 tbsp. lemon juice

2 tbsp. pine nuts, lightly toasted
2 scallions, finely chopped
salt and pepper

TO GARNISH:
ground cumin
2 tbsp. finely chopped fresh flat-leaf
   parsley

1 Using a fork or metal skewer, pierce the eggplants all over. Place them on a cookie sheet in a preheated oven at 450°F and roast for 20–25 minutes until they are very soft.

2 Use a folded dish towel to remove the eggplants from the cookie sheet and set aside to cool.

3 Place the tomato in a heatproof bowl, pour boiling water over to cover, and let stand for 30 seconds. Drain, then plunge into cold water to prevent it from cooking. Skin the tomato, then cut in half and scoop out the seeds with a teaspoon. Finely dice the flesh and set aside.

4 Cut the eggplants in half lengthwise. Scoop out the flesh with a spoon and transfer to a food processor. Add the garlic, olive oil, lemon juice, pine nuts, and salt and pepper to taste. Process until smooth.

5 Spoon the mixture into a bowl and stir through the scallions and diced tomato. Cover and chill for 30 minutes before serving.

6 Garnish the dip with a pinch of ground cumin and the finely chopped parsley, then serve.

VARIATION

Add 2–4 tablespoons tahini, to taste, in Step 4.

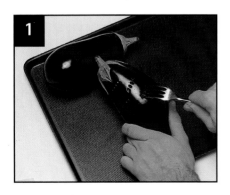

Tapenade

These robust olive and anchovy spreads can be as thick or as thin as you like.
They make flavorful appetizers spread on toasted slices of French bread or as dips for vegetables.

Each makes about 1 ¼ cups

INGREDIENTS

thin slices of day-old baguette (optional)
olive oil (optional)
finely chopped fresh flat-leaf parsley
    sprigs, to garnish

BLACK OLIVE TAPENADE:
9 oz. black Niçoise olives in brine, rinsed
    and pitted
1 large garlic clove
2 tbsp. walnut pieces

4 canned anchovy fillets, drained
about ½ cup extra-virgin olive oil
lemon juice, to taste
pepper

GREEN OLIVE TAPENADE:
9 oz. green olives in brine, rinsed and
    pitted
4 canned anchovy fillets, rinsed
4 tbsp. blanched almonds

1 tbsp. bottled capers in brine or vinegar,
    rinsed
about ½ cup extra-virgin olive oil
½–1 tbsp. finely grated orange rind
pepper

1 To make the black olive tapenade, put the olives, garlic, walnut pieces, and anchovies in a food processor and process until blended.

2 With the motor running, slowly add the olive oil through the feed tube, as if making mayonnaise. Add lemon juice and pepper to taste. Transfer to a bowl, cover with plastic wrap, and chill until required.

3 To make the green olive tapenade, put the olives, anchovies, almonds, and capers in a food processor and process until blended. With the motor running, slowly add the olive oil through the feed tube, as if making mayonnaise. Add orange rind, and pepper to taste. Transfer to a bowl, cover with plastic wrap, and chill until required.

4 To serve on croutons, if desired, toast the slices of bread on both sides until crisp. Brush one side of each slice with a little olive oil while they are still hot, so the oil is absorbed.

5 Spread the croutons with the tapenade of your choice and garnish with parsley.

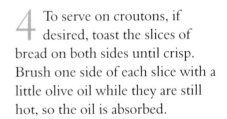

Bagna Cauda

Traditionally, this Italian hot anchovy dip is served in a special cup with a candle underneath to keep the dip warm while eating, but if this is not available you can always use a fondue burner instead.

Serves 4–6

INGREDIENTS

1¾ oz. cans anchovy fillets
  in oil
2 garlic cloves
5 tbsp. olive oil
6 tbsp. butter

TO SERVE:
red and green bell peppers
zucchini
carrots
small broccoli florets

1 Begin by preparing the vegetables for dipping. Cut the bell peppers in half, remove the cores and seeds and slice into ¼-inch strips. Cut the zucchini and carrots into ¼-inch strips. Place in a plastic bag and chill until required.

2 Drain the anchovy fillets, reserving 5 tablespoons of the oil. Then chop the anchovies and garlic. Put the anchovy oil and olive oil in a saucepan with the butter over high heat and stir until the butter melts.

3 Lower the heat to medium and add the garlic. Stir for 2 minutes, without letting it burn. Add the anchovies and allow them to simmer for about 10 minutes, stirring frequently, until they dissolve and turn the mixture into a thin paste.

4 Transfer the dip to a bagna cauda or fondue burner to keep it hot while you are eating. Serve with a platter of the prepared bell peppers, zucchini, carrots, and broccoli for dipping.

VARIATION

This full-flavored dip has a natural affinity with the sun-kissed vegetables from the Mediterranean, but you can serve it with any selection you like. Other suggestions include blanched white or green asparagus spears, blanched baby artichokes, blanched green beans, and cauliflower florets.

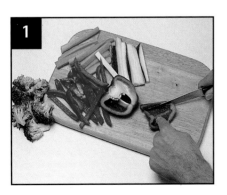

Iced Gazpacho

Anyone who has ever tasted this traditional Spanish soup on a hot summer's day will instantly understand why it is so popular throughout the Mediterranean. Its vibrant, refreshing flavors are unbeatable.

Serves 4–6

INGREDIENTS

2 ripe red bell peppers
1 cucumber
14 oz. large, juicy tomatoes, skinned, deseeded, and coarsely chopped
4 tbsp. olive oil
2 tbsp. sherry vinegar
salt and pepper

GARLIC CROUTONS:
2 tbsp. olive oil
1 garlic clove, halved
2 slices bread, crusts removed and cut into ¼-inch cubes
sea salt

TO GARNISH:
diced green bell pepper
diced red bell pepper
finely diced deseeded cucumber
chopped scallions
ice cubes

1 Cut the bell peppers in half and remove the cores and seeds, then coarsely chop. Peel the cucumber, cut it in half lengthwise, then cut into quarters. Remove the seeds with a teaspoon, then coarsely chop the flesh.

2 Put the bell peppers, cucumber, tomatoes, olive oil, and vinegar in a food processor and process until smooth. Season with salt and pepper to taste. Transfer to a bowl, cover, and chill for at least 4 hours.

3 Meanwhile, make the garlic croutons. Heat the oil in a skillet over medium-high heat. Add the garlic and fry, stirring, for 2 minutes to flavor the oil.

4 Remove and discard the garlic. Add the diced bread and fry until golden on all sides. Drain well on crumpled paper towels and sprinkle with sea salt. Store in an airtight container if not using at once.

5 To serve, place each of the vegetable garnishes in bowls for guests to add to their soup. Taste the soup and adjust the seasoning if necessary. Put ice cubes into soup bowls and ladle the soup on top. Serve at once.

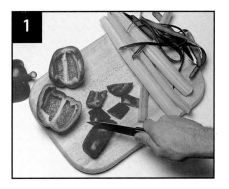

Chilled Garlic & Almond Soup

Do not let the idea of raw garlic cloves deter you from trying this—it's very refreshing. This is a Spanish recipe, but the combination of garlic and almonds is also popular in Greece and Turkey.

Serves 4–6

INGREDIENTS

14 oz. day-old French bread, sliced
4 large garlic cloves
3–4 tbsp. sherry vinegar
6 tbsp. extra-virgin olive oil

8 oz. ground almonds
4 cups water, chilled
sea salt and pepper

TO GARNISH:
seedless white grapes, chilled and sliced
pepper
extra-virgin olive oil

1 Tear the bread into small pieces and put in a bowl. Pour over enough cold water to cover and soak for 10–15 minutes. Using your hands, squeeze the bread dry. Transfer the bread to a food processor.

2 Cut the garlic cloves in half lengthwise and use the tip of the knife to remove the pale green or white cores. Add the garlic and 3 tablespoons of the sherry vinegar to the food processor with 1 cup of the water and process until blended. Add the oil and ground almonds and blend.

3 With the motor running, slowly pour in the remaining water until a smooth soup forms. Add extra sherry vinegar to taste, and season with salt and pepper. Transfer to a bowl, cover, and chill for at least 4 hours.

4 To serve, adjust the seasoning. Ladle into bowls and float grapes on top. Garnish each with a sprinkling of pepper and a swirl of olive oil. Serve while still cold.

COOK'S TIP

Chilled grapes are the traditional accompaniment for this, but many other ingredients are suitable. Serve with the Garlic Croutons and the diced vegetables suggested with the gazpacho recipe (see page 20). For garlic lovers, fry thin slices of garlic in olive oil until golden brown, then sprinkle over to add a crunchy contrast to the soup. Or, sprinkle with a light dusting of paprika or very finely chopped fresh parsley just before serving.

Avgolemono

The hallmarks of this traditional Greek lemon and egg soup are its fresh flavor and its lightness.
Serve accompanied with Olive Rolls (see page 202) for a first course or light lunch.

Serves 4–6

INGREDIENTS

5 cups homemade chicken
   stock
3½ oz. dried orzo, or other
   small pasta shapes

2 large eggs
4 tbsp. lemon juice
salt and pepper

TO GARNISH:
finely chopped fresh flat-leaf parsley

1 Pour the stock into a flame-proof casserole or heavy-based saucepan and bring to a boil. Sprinkle in the orzo, return to a boil and cook for 8–10 minutes, or according to packet instructions, until the pasta is tender.

2 Whisk the eggs in a bowl, for at least 30 seconds. Add the lemon juice and continue whisking for a further 30 seconds.

3 Reduce the heat under the pan of stock and orzo until the stock is not boiling.

4 Very slowly add 4–5 tablespoons of the hot (not boiling) stock to the lemon and egg mixture, whisking constantly. Slowly add another 1 cup of the stock, whisking to prevent the eggs from curdling.

5 Slowly pour the lemon and egg mixture into the pan, whisking until the soup thickens slightly. Do not allow it to boil. Season with salt and pepper.

6 Spoon the soup into warmed soup bowls and sprinkle

with chopped flat-leaf parsley. Serve at once.

VARIATION

To make a more substantial soup, add 2 cups finely chopped cooked, skinless chicken meat. This version uses orzo, a small pasta shape that looks like barley grains, but you can substitute long-grain rice.

Roasted Bell Pepper & Tomato Soup with Dill

Ripe, juicy tomatoes and sweet red bell peppers are roasted to enhance their delicious flavors, then combined with fresh dill and orange to make a fantastic soup.

Serves 6–8

INGREDIENTS

2 lb. 4 oz. juicy plum tomatoes, halved

2 large red bell peppers, cored, deseeded and halved

1 onion, quartered

3 sprigs fresh dill, tied together, plus a little extra to garnish

1 thin piece of orange rind

juice of 1 orange

2½ cups vegetable stock

1–1½ tbsp. red wine vinegar

salt and pepper

Mediterranean Bread (see page 198), to serve

1 Place the tomatoes and peppers on a cookie sheet, cut-sides up to catch the juices. Add the onion quarters. Place in a preheated oven at 450°F and roast for 20–25 minutes until the vegetables just start to char on the edges.

2 As the vegetables become charred, transfer them to a large flameproof casserole or stockpot. Add the dill, orange rind and juice, stock, and salt and pepper to taste. Bring to a boil.

3 Lower the heat, partially cover and simmer for 25 minutes. Remove the bundle of dill and transfer the rest of the ingredients to a food mill (see Cook's Tip) and puree. Alternatively, process in a food processor and work though a strainer.

4 Return the soup to the rinsed casserole or stockpot and reheat. Stir in the vinegar and adjust the seasoning with salt and pepper, if necessary. Ladle into bowls and garnish with extra dill. Serve hot, with slices of Mediterranean Bread.

COOK'S TIP

A food mill, or mouli-legume as it is called in France, is ideal for pureeing vegetable soups and sauces because it removes the skin and seeds in the process.

Pistou

This hearty soup of beans and vegetables is from Nice and gets its name from the fresh basil sauce stirred in at the last minute. The basil will fill your kitchen with a tantalizing aroma.

Serves 6–8

INGREDIENTS

2 young carrots
2 potatoes
7 oz. fresh peas in the shells
7 oz. thin green beans
5½ oz. young zucchini
2 tbsp. olive oil
1 garlic clove, crushed
1 large onion, finely chopped

10 cups vegetable stock or
  water
1 bouquet garni of 2 sprigs fresh
  parsley and 1 bay leaf tied in a
  3-inch piece of celery
3 oz. dried small soup pasta
1 large tomato, skinned, deseeded, and
  chopped or diced

pared Parmesan cheese, to serve

PISTOU SAUCE:
1½ cups fresh basil leaves
1 garlic clove
5 tbsp. fruity extra-virgin olive oil
salt and pepper

1 To make the pistou sauce, put the basil leaves, garlic, and olive oil in a food processor and process until well blended. Season with salt and pepper to taste. Transfer to a bowl, cover, and chill until required.

2 Peel the carrots and cut them in half lengthwise, then slice. Peel the potatoes and cut into quarters lengthwise, then slice. Set aside.

3 Shell the peas. Trim the ends from the beans and cut them into 1-inch pieces. Cut the zucchini in half lengthwise, then slice.

4 Heat the oil in a large saucepan or flameproof casserole. Add the garlic and fry for 2 minutes, stirring. Add the onion and continue frying for 2 minutes until soft. Add the carrots and potatoes and stir for about 30 seconds.

5 Pour in the stock and bring to a boil. Lower the heat, partially cover, and simmer for 8 minutes, until the vegetables are starting to become tender.

6 Stir in the peas, beans, zucchini, bouquet garni, and pasta. Season and cook for 4 minutes, or until the vegetables and pasta are tender. Stir in the pistou or sauce and serve with Parmesan.

Prosciutto Ham with Fruit

In this classic Italian appetizer, the slightly salty flavor of air-cured prosciutto ham provides a marvelous contrast to the sweet fresh fruit.

Serves 4

INGREDIENTS

1 cantaloupe or honeydew melon
4 ripe fresh figs (optional)

12 wafer-thin slices prosciutto ham

olive oil, to drizzle
pepper
fresh parsley sprigs, to garnish

1 Cut the melon in half lengthwise. Using a spoon, scoop out the seeds and discard them. Cut each half into 8 thin wedges. Using a paring knife, cut the rind off each slice.

2 Cut the stems off the figs, if using, but do not peel them. Stand the figs upright with the pointed end upward. Cut each into quarters without cutting all the way through, so you can open them out into attractive "flowers."

3 Arrange 3–4 slices of prosciutto on individual serving plates and top with the melon slices and fig "flowers," if using. Alternatively, arrange the melon slices on the plates and completely cover with the prosciutto; add the figs, if using.

4 Drizzle with olive oil, then grind a little pepper over the top. Garnish with parsley and serve at once.

COOK'S TIP

For an attractive presentation, you can also prepare all the ingredients on one large serving platter and let guests help themselves.

VARIATION

For a Spanish flavor, replace the prosciutto with Serrano ham, which also has a slightly salty flavor but is rarely cut as finely.

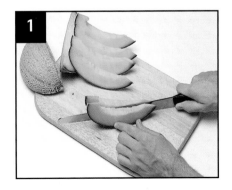

Chorizo & Chickpea Tapas

A glass of chilled sherry and a selection of Spanish tapas is a great way to unwind at the end of the day. This simple salad is typical of the tapas served at Spanish seaside resorts around Barcelona.

Serves 4

INGREDIENTS

7 tbsp. olive oil
about 2 tbsp. sherry vinegar
9 oz. fresh chorizo sausage,
   in one piece

1 small Spanish onion, chopped finely
14 oz. can chickpeas
salt and pepper

finely chopped fresh oregano or flat-
   leaf parsley, to garnish
chunks of fresh bread, to serve

1 Place 6 tablespoons of the olive oil and 2 tablespoons of the vinegar in a bowl and whisk together. Taste and add a little more sherry vinegar, if desired. Season with salt and pepper and set aside.

2 Using a small, sharp knife, remove the casing from the chorizo sausage. Cut the meat into ¼-inch thick slices, then cut each slice into half-moon shapes.

3 Heat the remaining olive oil in a small skillet over medium-high heat. Add the onion and fry for 2–3 minutes, stirring. Add the chorizo sausage and cook for 3 minutes, or until the sausage is cooked through.

4 Using a slotted spoon, remove the sausage and onion and drain on crumpled paper towels. Transfer to the bowl with the dressing while still hot and stir together.

5 Empty the chickpeas into a colander and rinse well under running water; shake off the excess water. Add to the bowl with the other ingredients and stir together. Let cool.

6 Just before serving, adjust the seasoning, then spoon the salad into a serving bowl and sprinkle with chopped herbs. Serve with chunks of fresh bread.

Dolmas

Start a Greek meal with these vegetarian stuffed grape leaves. You will need a large skillet with a lid, that can hold all the stuffed grape leaves in a single layer.

Makes 25–30

INGREDIENTS

8 oz. package grape leaves preserved in brine, about 40 in total
²/₃ cup olive oil
4 tbsp. lemon juice
1¼ cups water
lemon wedges, to serve

FILLING:
generous ½ cup long-grain rice, not basmati
1½ cups water
½ cup currants
2 oz. pine nuts, chopped
2 scallions, very finely chopped

4 tbsp. very finely chopped fresh parsley
1 tbsp. very finely chopped fresh cilantro
1 tbsp. very finely chopped fresh parsley
1 tbsp. very finely chopped fresh dill
finely grated rind of ½ lemon

1 Rinse the grape leaves and place them in a heatproof bowl. Pour over enough boiling water to cover and soak for 5 minutes. Drain well.

2 Meanwhile, place the rice and water in a pan with a pinch of salt and bring to a boil. Lower the heat, cover, and simmer for 10–12 minutes, or until all the liquid is absorbed. Drain and let cool.

3 Stir the currants, pine nuts, scallions, herbs, and lemon rind into the cooled rice. Season well with salt and pepper.

4 Line the bottom of a large skillet with 3 or 4 of the thickest grape leaves, or any that are torn.

5 Put a grape leaf on the work surface, vein-side upward, with

the pointed end facing away from you. Put a small, compact roll of the stuffing at the base of the leaf. Fold up the bottom end of the leaf.

6 Fold in each side to overlap in the center. Roll up the leaf around the filling. Squeeze lightly in your hand. Continue this process with the remaining leaves.

7 Place the leaf rolls in a single layer in the pan, seam-side down. Combine the olive oil, lemon juice, and water and pour into the pan.

8 Fit a heatproof plate over the rolls and cover the pan. Simmer for 30 minutes. Remove from the heat and leave the stuffed grape leaves to cool in the liquid. Serve chilled with lemon wedges.

Grilled Sardines

When you drive along the Mediterranean coast, you'll come across small harbor-side restaurants broiling the day's catch of sardines.

Serves 4–6

INGREDIENTS

12 sardines
olive oil
fresh flat-leaf parsley sprigs, to
   garnish
lemon wedges, to serve

DRESSING:
²/₃ cup extra-virgin olive oil
finely grated rind of 1 large lemon
4 tbsp. lemon juice, or to taste
4 shallots, thinly sliced

1 small fresh red chili, deseeded and
   finely chopped
1 large garlic clove, finely chopped
salt and pepper

1 To make the dressing, place all the ingredients in a screw-top jar, season with salt and pepper, then shake until blended. Pour into a non-metallic baking dish that is large enough to hold the sardines in a single layer. Set aside.

2 To prepare the sardines, chop off the heads and make a slit all along the length of each belly. Pull out the insides, rinse the fish inside and out with cold water, and pat dry with paper towels.

3 Line the broiler pan with foil, shiny side up. Brush the foil with a little olive oil to prevent the sardines from sticking. Arrange the sardines on the foil in a single layer and brush with a little of the dressing. Broil under a preheated broiler for about 90 seconds.

4 Turn the fish over, brush with a little more dressing, and continue broiling for 90 seconds, or until they are cooked through and flake easily.

5 Transfer the fish to the dish with the dressing. Spoon the dressing over the fish and cool completely. Cover and chill for at least 2 hours to allow the flavors to blend.

6 Transfer the sardines to a serving platter and garnish with parsley. Serve with lemon wedges for squeezing over.

Ceviche

This no-cook seafood salad is popular throughout the Mediterranean where freshly caught fish and shellfish are plentiful. It is essential to use ultra-fresh seafood for this dish.

Serves 4

INGREDIENTS

8 fresh scallops
16 large shrimp in shells
2 sea bass fillets, about 5½ oz. each,
  skinned
1 large lemon

1 lime
1 red onion, thinly sliced
½ red chili, deseeded and finely
  chopped
2–4 tbsp. extra-virgin olive oil

TO SERVE:
salad leaves
lime or lemon wedges
pepper

1 If the scallops are in shells, use an oyster knife or small knife to pry the shells open, then rinse under running cold water. Cut the scallop flesh and coral free from the shells. Slice the flesh into 2 or 3 horizontal slices each, depending on the size. Place in a non-metallic bowl with the corals.

2 Cut the heads off the shrimp, then peel off the shells. Using a small sharp knife, make a thin slice all along the back of the shrimp. Use the tip of the knife to

remove the thin black vein. Add to the scallops.

3 Cut the sea bass into thin slices across the grain and add to the shellfish.

4 Firmly roll the lemon and lime backward and forward on a work surface. Cut the lemon in half and squeeze the juice over the fish. Repeat with the lime.

5 Gently stir, to coat the seafood well in the citrus juices, then

cover and chill for 2 hours, or until the seafood becomes opaque, but do not leave for longer—otherwise the seafood will be too soft.

6 Using a slotted spoon, transfer the seafood to a bowl. Add the onion, chili, and olive oil and gently stir together. Let stand for 5 minutes.

7 Spoon onto individual plates and serve with salad leaves, lemon or lime wedges, and black pepper.

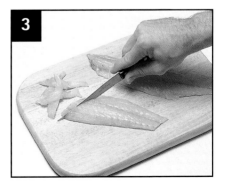

Crab & Celery Root Remoulade

Finely shredded celery root in a mustard-flavored mayonnaise is a popular dish throughout France, but here it is given a Provençal touch with fresh crab meat and capers.

Serves 4

INGREDIENTS

1¹/₂ tsp. lemon juice
1 tsp. salt
1 lb. celery root
1¹/₂ tbsp. Dijon mustard
1 large egg yolk

²/₃ cup extra-virgin olive oil
2 tsp. white wine vinegar
2 tbsp. capers in brine, rinsed
10¹/₂ oz. fresh crab meat

radicchio leaves, rinsed and dried, to serve
fresh dill or parsley sprigs, to garnish

1 Put the lemon juice and salt in a bowl of water. Using the shredding disc of a food processor or a hand grater, shred the celery root. Put the celery root in the bowl of acidulated water as it is grated, to prevent discoloration.

2 To make the sauce, beat the mustard and egg yolk together in a bowl. Gradually whisk in the olive oil, drop by drop, until a mayonnaise forms (see Cook's Tip). Stir in the vinegar.

3 Drain the celery root and pat dry with paper towels. Add to the mayonnaise, stirring to coat well. Cover and chill.

4 About 20 minutes before serving, remove the remoulade from the refrigerator to allow it to come to room temperature. Stir in the capers and crab meat.

5 Line a platter or bowl with radicchio leaves and spoon the remoulade mixture on top. Garnish with dill or parsley and serve.

COOK'S TIP

If the sauce begins to curdle, beat another egg yolk in a bowl, then slowly beat into the sauce to rectify. Continue to add the remaining oil.

Greek Salad

The combination of juicy, ripe tomatoes and black olives is a classic partnership in Mediterranean cooking, but Greek cooks also add feta cheese for a contrasting salty flavor.

Serves 4

INGREDIENTS

9 oz. feta cheese	4 tbsp. extra-virgin olive oil
9 oz. cucumber	½ lemon
9 oz. Greek kalamata olives	salt and pepper
1 red onion or 4 scallions	fresh or dried oregano, to garnish
2 large juicy tomatoes	pita bread, to serve
1 tsp. honey	

1 Drain the feta cheese if it is packed in brine. Place it on a chopping board and cut into ½-inch cubes. Transfer to a salad bowl.

2 Cut the cucumber in half lengthwise and use a teaspoon to scoop out the seeds. Cut the flesh into ½-inch slices. Add to the bowl with the feta cheese.

3 Pit the olives with an olive or cherry pitter and add them to the salad bowl. Slice the red onion or finely chop the white and green parts of the scallions, and add to the salad bowl.

4 Cut each tomato into quarters and scoop out the seeds with a teaspoon. Cut the flesh into bite-sized pieces and add to the bowl.

5 Using your hands, gently toss all the ingredients together. Stir the honey into the olive oil (see Cook's Tip), add to the salad and squeeze in lemon juice to taste. Season with pepper and a little salt, if wished. Cover and chill until required.

6 Garnish with the oregano and serve with pita bread.

COOK'S TIP

The small amount of honey helps to bring out the full flavor of the tomatoes.

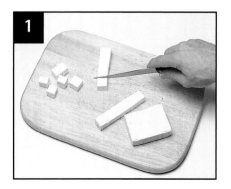

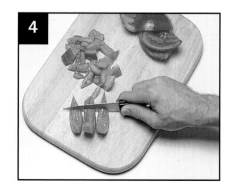

Baked Goat's Cheese Salad

Scrumptious hot goat's cheese and herb croutons are served with a tossed leafy salad to make an excellent light snack, capturing Provençal flavors.

Serves 4

INGREDIENTS

9 oz. mixed salad leaves, such as
    arugula and endive
12 slices French bread
extra-virgin olive oil, for
    brushing
12 thin slices of Provençal goat's
    cheese, such as Picodon

fresh herbs, such as rosemary, thyme,
    or oregano, finely chopped
extra French bread, to serve

DRESSING:
6 tbsp. extra-virgin olive oil
3 tbsp. red wine vinegar
1/2 tsp. sugar
1/2 tsp. Dijon mustard
salt and pepper

1 To prepare the salad, rinse the leaves under cold water and pat dry with a dish towel. Wrap in paper towels and put in a plastic bag. Seal tightly and chill until required.

2 To make the dressing, place all the ingredients in a screw-top jar and shake until well blended. Season with salt and pepper to taste and shake again. Set aside while preparing the croutons.

3 Toast the slices of bread on both sides until they are crisp. Brush a little olive oil on one side of each slice while still hot, so the oil is absorbed.

4 Place the croutons on a cookie sheet and top each with a slice of cheese. Sprinkle the herbs over the cheese and drizzle with olive oil. Bake in a preheated oven at 350°F for 5 minutes.

5 While the croutons are in the oven, place the salad leaves in a bowl. Shake the dressing again, pour it over the leaves, and toss together. Equally divide the salad between 4 plates.

6 Transfer the hot croutons to the salads. Serve at once with extra slices of French bread.

Orange & Fennel Salad

Fresh, juicy oranges and the sharp aniseed flavor of fennel combine to make this refreshing Spanish salad.
Serve before a rich main course, or as a light lunch with plenty of French bread.

Serves 4

INGREDIENTS

4 large oranges
1 large bulb fennel
2 tsp. fennel seeds
2 tbsp. extra-virgin olive oil

freshly squeezed orange juice, to taste
finely chopped fresh parsley,
    to garnish

1 Using a small serrated knife, remove the rind and pith from one orange, cutting carefully from the top to the bottom of the orange so it retains its shape. Work over a bowl to catch the juices.

2 Peel the remaining oranges the same way, reserving all the juices. Cut the oranges horizontally into ¼-inch slices and arrange in an attractive serving bowl; reserve the juices.

3 Place the fennel bulb on a chopping board and cut off the fronds. Cut the bulb in half lengthwise and then into quarters. Cut crosswise into the thinnest slices you can manage. Immediately transfer to the bowl with the oranges and toss with a little of the reserved orange juice to prevent browning.

4 Sprinkle the fennel seeds over the oranges and fennel.

5 Place the olive oil in a small bowl and whisk in the rest of the reserved orange juice, plus extra fresh orange juice to taste. Pour over the oranges and fennel and toss gently. Cover with plastic wrap and chill until ready to serve.

6 Just before serving, remove from the refrigerator and sprinkle with parsley. Serve chilled.

VARIATION

Replace the fennel with a finely sliced onion or a large bunch of scallions, finely chopped. This version is from Spain, where orange-colored oranges would be used, but in Sicily the dish is made with blood-red oranges.

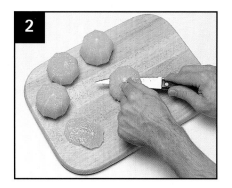
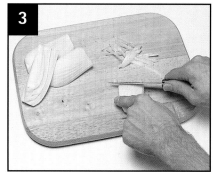

Spanish Tortilla

This simple recipe transforms the most humble ingredients—potatoes, eggs and an onion—into a delicious thick omelet, ideal to serve as part of tapas, or as a light lunch.

Serves 6–8

INGREDIENTS

$^1\!/_2$ cup olive oil

1 lb. 4 oz. potatoes, sliced

1 large onion, sliced

1 large garlic clove, crushed

6 large eggs

salt and pepper

1 Heat a 10-inch skillet, preferably non-stick, over high heat. Pour in the oil and heat. Lower the heat, add the potatoes, onion, and garlic and cook for 15–20 minutes, stirring frequently, until the potatoes are tender.

2 Beat the eggs together in a large bowl and season generously with salt and pepper. Using a slotted spoon, transfer the potatoes and onion to the bowl of eggs. Pour the excess oil left in the skillet into a heatproof pitcher, then scrape off the crusty bits from the base of the pan.

3 Reheat the pan. Add about 2 tablespoons of the reserved oil reserved in the pitcher. Pour in the potato mixture, smoothing the vegetables into an even layer. Cook for about 5 minutes, shaking the pan occasionally, or until the base is set.

4 Shake the pan and use a spatula to loosen the side of the tortilla. Place a large plate over the pan. Carefully invert the tortilla onto the plate.

5 If you are not using a non-stick pan, add 1 tablespoon of the reserved oil to the pan and swirl around. Gently slide the tortilla back into the pan, cooked-side up. Use the spatula to "tuck down" the side. Continue cooking over medium heat for 3–5 minutes until set.

6 Remove the pan from the heat and slide the tortilla onto a serving plate. Let it cool for at least 5 minutes before cutting. Serve hot, warm, or at room temperature with salad.

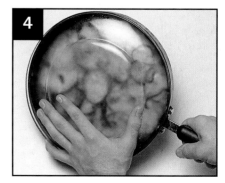

Spinach, Onion, & Herb Frittata

It you find the prospect of turning over a Spanish Tortilla (see page 48) daunting, try this Italian version of a flat omelet, that finishes cooking under a broiler.

Serves 6–8

INGREDIENTS

4 tbsp. olive oil
6 scallions, sliced
9 oz. young spinach leaves, any coarse
   stems removed, rinsed

6 large eggs
3 tbsp. finely chopped mixed fresh
   herbs, such as flat-leaf parsley,
   thyme, and cilantro

2 tbsp. freshly grated Parmesan
   cheese, plus extra for garnishing
salt and pepper
fresh parsley sprigs, to garnish

1 Heat a 10-inch skillet, preferably non-stick with a flameproof handle, over medium heat. Add the oil and heat. Add the scallions and fry for about 2 minutes. Add the spinach with only the water clinging to its leaves and cook until it wilts.

2 Beat the eggs together in a large bowl and season generously with salt and pepper. Using a slotted spoon, transfer the spinach and onions to the bowl of eggs and stir in the herbs. Pour the excess oil left in the skillet into a heat-proof pitcher, then scrape off the crusty bits from the base of the pan.

3 Reheat the pan. Add 2 tablespoons of the reserved oil. Pour in the egg mixture, smoothing it into an even layer. Cook for 6 minutes, shaking the pan occasionally, or until the base is set when you lift up the side with a spatula.

4 Sprinkle the top of the frittata with the Parmesan. Place the pan below a preheated broiler and cook for about 3 minutes, or until the excess liquid is set and the cheese is golden.

5 Remove the pan from the heat and slide the tortilla onto a serving plate. Let it cool for at least 5 minutes before cutting and garnishing with extra Parmesan and parsley. Serve hot, warm, or at room temperature.

Piperade

Serve this rustic egg and bell pepper dish to add a Mediterranean flavor to a light lunch. It's particularly good with prosciutto.

Serves 4–6

INGREDIENTS

2 tbsp. olive oil
1 large onion, finely chopped
1 large red bell pepper, cored, deseeded, and sliced
1 large yellow bell pepper, cored, deseeded, and sliced

1 large green bell pepper
8 large eggs
salt and pepper
2 tomatoes, deseeded and chopped
2 tbsp. finely chopped fresh flat-leaf parsley

4–6 slices thick country-style bread, toasted, to serve
fresh flat-leaf parsley sprigs, to garnish

1 Heat the olive oil in a saucepan over a medium-high heat. Add the onion and peppers, lower the heat, and cook slowly for 15–20 minutes until they are soft.

2 Meanwhile, place the eggs in a mixing bowl and whisk until well blended. Season with salt and pepper to taste. Set aside.

3 When the peppers are soft, pour the eggs into the pan and cook, stirring constantly, over very low heat until they are almost set but still creamy. Remove from the heat.

4 Stir in the chopped tomatoes and chopped parsley. Adjust the seasoning, if necessary. Place the pieces of toast on individual plates and spoon the eggs and vegetables on top. Garnish with sprigs of parsley and serve at once.

COOK'S TIP

To make this dish more substantial, serve with thickly cut slices of Serrano ham from Spain or prosciutto from Italy. The salty taste of both contrasts well with the sweetness of the peppers.

Lemon Risotto

This is a stylish first course, with an aroma and fresh taste that stimulates the taste buds for the meal to follow.

Serves 4

INGREDIENTS

2–3 lemons
2 tbsp. olive oil
2 shallots, finely chopped
1½ cups risotto rice
½ cup dry white
 vermouth

4 cups vegetable or chicken stock,
 simmering
1 tbsp. very finely chopped fresh flat-
 leaf parsley
2 tbsp. butter

freshly pared Parmesan cheese, to
 serve

TO GARNISH:
thin strips of pared lemon rind
fresh parsley sprigs

1 Finely grate the rind from 2 lemons. Firmly roll the rindless lemons backward and forward on a board, then squeeze a scant ½ cup juice. If you don't have enough, squeeze another lemon. Set the rind and juice aside.

2 Heat the olive oil in a heavy-based saucepan. Add the shallots and fry, stirring, for about 3 minutes until soft. Add the rice and stir until all the grains are well coated.

3 Stir in the vermouth and let it bubble until it evaporates. Lower the heat to medium-low. Add the lemon juice and a ladleful of simmering stock. Stir together, then let simmer, only stirring occasionally, until all the liquid is absorbed.

4 Add another ladleful of stock and stir, then simmer until absorbed. Continue adding stock in this way, allowing it to be absorbed after each addition, until all the stock has been used and the risotto is creamy, with several tablespoons of liquid floating on the surface.

5 Stir in the lemon rind and parsley. Add the butter, cover, remove from the heat, and let it stand for 5 minutes. Stir well and then garnish with lemon strips and parsley. Serve with Parmesan cheese and avocado slices.

Pissaladière

This Provençal onion tart also includes anchovies and olives.
Robustly flavored, it makes a delicious light lunch served with green salad.

Serves 6–8

INGREDIENTS

about 6 tbsp. olive oil

3 large garlic cloves, crushed

2 lb. 4 oz. onions, thinly sliced

3–4 tbsp. Black Olive Tapenade (see page 16)

1³/₄ oz. can anchovy fillets in oil, drained and halved lengthwise

12 black olives, such as Niçoise, or Flavored Olives (see page 172), pitted

finely chopped fresh flat-leaf parsley, to garnish

CRUST:

1¹/₄ cups all-purpose flour

pinch of salt

6 tbsp. butter, diced

2–3 tbsp. ice-cold water

1 To make the pastry crust, put the flour and salt in a bowl; stir. Rub the butter into the flour until fine crumbs form. Add 2 tablespoons of the water to make a dough. Only add the extra water if necessary. Lightly knead the dough, then shape into a ball, wrap in plastic wrap and chill for at least 1 hour.

2 Heat the oil in a large skillet with a tight-fitting lid. Add the garlic and stir for 2 minutes.

Add the onions and stir to coat in oil. Turn the heat to its lowest setting.

3 Dip a piece of waxed paper, large enough to fit over the top of the pan, in water. Shake off the excess and press it onto the onions. Cover with the lid and cook for 45 minutes, or until tender.

4 Meanwhile, roll out the dough on a lightly floured

surface and use to line a 8-inch tart pan with a removable base. Prick all over and line with waxed paper and baking beans. Chill for 10 minutes.

5 Bake the lined pastry shell on a hot cookie sheet in a preheated oven at 425°F for 15 minutes. Remove the paper and bake for a further 5 minutes. Lower the oven to 350°F.

6 Spread the olive paste over the baked pastry shell. Fill the shell with the onions. Arrange the anchovy fillets in a lattice pattern and scatter the olives over the top.

7 Bake for 25–30 minutes. Stand for 10 minutes before removing from the pan. Scatter with the parsley and serve.

Spanakopitas

These Greek spinach and feta pies, encased in layers of crisp filo pastry, are often made in one large pan, but individual ones are ideal to serve as a first course.

Serves 4

INGREDIENTS

2 tbsp. olive oil

6 scallions, chopped

9 oz. fresh young spinach leaves, tough stems removed, rinsed

1/4 cup long-grain rice (not basmati), boiled until tender, and drained

4 tbsp. chopped fresh dill

4 tbsp. chopped fresh parsley

4 tbsp. pine nuts

2 tbsp. raisins

2 oz. feta cheese, drained if necessary and crumbled

1 nutmeg

pinch of cayenne pepper (optional)

40 sheets filo pastry

about 1 cup plus 2 tbsp. melted butter

pepper

1 Heat the oil in a pan, add the scallions, and fry for about 2 minutes. Add the spinach, with just the water clinging to the leaves, and cook, stirring, until the leaves wilt. Transfer to a bowl and, when cool enough to handle, squeeze dry.

2 Stir in the rice, herbs, pine nuts, raisins, and feta cheese. Grate in one-quarter of the nutmeg, and add black and cayenne peppers to taste.

3 Leave the filo sheets in a stack. Cut forty 6-inch squares. Remove 8 slices and cut into eight 4-inch circles. Re-wrap the unused pastry and cover the squares and circles with a damp dish towel.

4 Brush a 4-inch tart pan with a removable base with butter. Place in one square of filo and brush with more butter. Repeat with 7 more sheets. Do not push the filo into the ridges.

5 Spoon in one-quarter of the filling and smooth the surface. Top with a filo circle and brush with butter. Repeat with another filo circle. Fold the over-hanging filo over the top and brush with butter. Make 3 more pies.

6 Put the pies on a cookie sheet and bake in a preheated oven at 350°F for 20–25 minutes until crisp and golden. Let stand for 5 minutes before removing from cookie sheet.

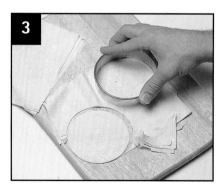

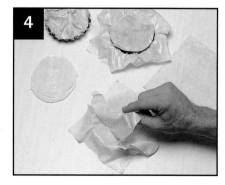

Tuna & Tomato Boreks

In Turkey, these delicate filo-wrapped snacks would usually have a filling made with the day's local catch, but elsewhere canned tuna will do!

Makes about 18 boreks

INGREDIENTS

about 18 sheets filo pastry, each
    15 x 6 inches, defrosted if frozen
vegetable oil, for shallow frying
sea salt, to garnish
lemon wedges, to serve

FILLING:
2 hard-boiled eggs, shelled and finely
    chopped
7 oz. canned tuna in brine, drained
1 tbsp. chopped fresh dill

1 tomato, skinned, deseeded, and very
    finely chopped
1/4 tsp. cayenne pepper
salt and pepper

1 To make the filling, put the eggs in a bowl with the tuna and dill. Mash the mixture until blended.

2 Stir in the tomato, taking care not to break it up too much. Season with the cayenne and salt and pepper to taste. Set aside.

3 Place one sheet of filo pastry on the work surface with a short side nearest to you; keep the remaining sheets covered with a damp dish towel. Arrange about 1 tablespoon of the filling in a line along the short side, about ½ inch in from the end and 1 inch in from both long sides.

4 Make one tight roll to enclose the filling, then fold in both long sides for the length of the filo. Continue rolling up to the end. Use a little vegetable oil to seal the end. Repeat to make 17 more rolls, or until all the filling has been used up.

5 Heat 1 inch oil in a skillet to 350–375°F, or until a cube of day-old bread browns in 30 seconds. Fry 2–3 boreks at a time, until they are golden brown all over. Drain well on crumpled paper towels and sprinkle with sea salt. Serve hot or at room temperature with lemon wedges.

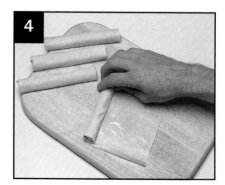

Pizza Biancas with Zucchini

Simple, fresh flavors are the highlight of this thin pizza. For the best results, use buffalo mozzarella imported from Italy, and avoid the mass-produced version made with cow's milk.

Makes two 9-inch pizzas

INGREDIENTS

scant 3 cups all-purpose flour,
plus extra for rolling
and dusting
1 envelope active dry yeast

1 tsp. salt
1 tbsp. extra-virgin olive oil, plus extra
for greasing

TOPPING:
2 zucchini
$10^{1}/_{2}$ oz. buffalo mozzarella
$1^{1}/_{2}$–2 tbsp. finely chopped fresh
rosemary, or $^{1}/_{2}$ tbsp. dried

1 To make the crust, heat 1 cup water in the microwave on High for 1 minute, or until it reads 125°F on an instant-read thermometer.

2 Stir the flour, yeast, and salt together and make a well in the center. Stir in most of the water with the olive oil to make a dough. Add the remaining water, if necessary, to form a soft dough.

3 Turn out onto a lightly floured surface and knead for about 10 minutes until smooth but still soft.

Wash the bowl and lightly coat with olive oil. Shape the dough into a ball, put in the bowl and turn the dough over so it is coated. Cover and leave until doubled in size.

4 Turn the dough out onto a lightly floured surface. Quickly knead a few times, then cover with the upturned bowl and leave for 10 minutes.

5 Meanwhile, using a vegetable peeler, cut long, thin strips of zucchini. Drain and dice the mozzarella.

6 Divide the dough in half and shape each half into a ball. Cover one ball and roll out the other one into a 9-inch circle. Place the circle on a lightly floured cookie sheet.

7 Scatter half the mozzarella over the base. Add half the zucchini strips and sprinkle with half the rosemary. Repeat with the remaining dough.

8 Bake in a preheated oven at 425°F for 15 minutes, or until crispy.

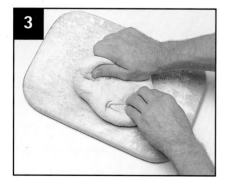

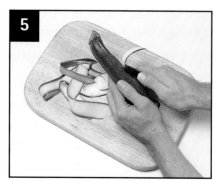

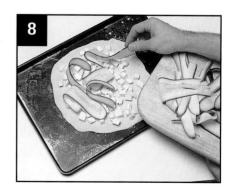

Pan Bagna

A cornucopia of the best flavors of the Mediterranean, this French sandwich never follows a set recipe. Treat this version as a suggestion and use your favorite ingredients for the filling.

Serves 4

INGREDIENTS

16-inch long loaf of country bread, thicker than a French baguette	FILLING:	lettuce or arugula leaves, rinsed and patted dry
fruity extra-virgin olive oil	2 eggs	about 4 plum tomatoes, sliced
Black or Green Olive Tapenade (see page 16) (optional)	1¾ oz. anchovy fillets in oil	7 oz. can tuna in brine, well drained and flaked
	about 3 oz. Flavored Olives of your choice (see page 172)	

1 To make the filling, start by hard-boiling the eggs. Bring a saucepan of water to a boil. Add the eggs and return to a boil, then continue boiling for 12 minutes. Drain and immediately plunge into a bowl of ice-cold water to stop the cooking.

2 Shell the cooked eggs and cut into slices. Drain the anchovy fillets well, then cut them in half lengthwise if large. Pit the olives and slice in half. Set aside.

3 Using a serrated knife, slice the loaf in half lengthwise. Remove about ½-inch of the crumb from the top and bottom, leaving a border all around both halves.

4 Generously brush both halves with the olive oil. Spread with tapenade, if you like a strong, robust flavor. Arrange a layer of lettuce or arugula leaves on the bottom half.

5 Add layers of hard-boiled egg slices, tomato slices, olives, anchovies, and tuna, sprinkling with olive oil and adding lettuce or arugula leaves between the layers. Make the filling as thick as you like.

6 Place the other bread half on top and press down firmly. Wrap tightly in plastic wrap and place on a board or plate that will fit in your refrigerator. Weight down and chill for several hours. To serve, slice into 4 equal portions, tying with string to secure in place, if desired.

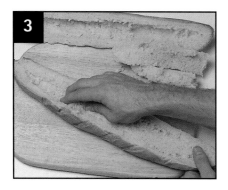

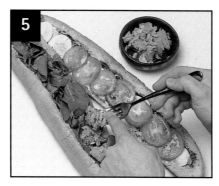

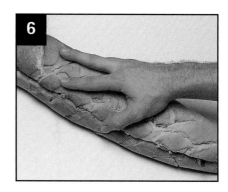

Olive Cake

This simple savory cake makes a delicious snack to nibble with a chilled glass of sparkling wine.
It keeps fresh for two days in an airtight container.

Makes 12–15 slices

INGREDIENTS

9 oz. pitted black or green olives,
   or a mixture
2 cups plus 2 tbsp. self-rising
   flour

4 large eggs
1 tbsp. superfine sugar
$\frac{1}{2}$ cup milk
$\frac{1}{2}$ cup olive oil

butter, for greasing
salt and pepper

1 Lightly butter a 8-inch cake pan, 2 inches deep. Line the base with a piece of waxed paper cut to fit. Put the olives in a small bowl and toss in 2 tablespoons of the measured flour.

2 Break the eggs into a bowl and lightly whisk. Stir in the sugar and season with salt and pepper to taste. Stir in the milk and olive oil.

3 Sift the flour into the bowl, add the coated olives, and stir together. Spoon the mixture into the prepared pan and smooth the surface.

4 Bake in a preheated oven at 400°F for 45 minutes. Lower the oven temperature to 325°F and continue baking for 15 minutes until the cake is risen, golden, and coming away from the side of the pan.

5 Remove from the oven and let cool in the pan on a wire rack for 20 minutes. Remove from the pan, peel off the lining paper, and let cool completely. Store in an airtight container.

COOK'S TIP

Serve this with
Black Olive Tapenade
(see page 16) for spreading,
or as part of an antipasti platter
with a selection of cooked meats.

Main Courses

The seemingly endless variety of fish and shellfish from Mediterranean waters means you always enjoy delicious seafood meals in the region. Each country "personalizes" the dishes with different flavors, but all Mediterranean cooks rely on freshly caught ingredients in the best condition. Mouthwatering dishes combining shellfish and fish are a specialty and the Seafood Stew is a classic example—delicately flavored with saffron, it immediately conjures up images of a sun-drenched harbor-side restaurant. For a taste of heartier Mediterranean flavors, try Seared Tuna with Anchovy & Orange Butter, or pan-fried red mullet wrapped in grape leaves. Few dishes can be easier to prepare than Mediterranean Monkfish, where the sweet white fish is paired with cherry tomatoes and pesto sauce.

But seafood isn't the only ingredient you will find on menus. The Italians love their tender veal—Vitello Tonnato is a divine combination of veal and tuna—while the Greeks, Turks, and Moroccans always cook lamb, often broiled with herbs. Pigs, not expensive to rear, are also turned into hearty dishes, often transforming the most inexpensive cuts into succulent meals, such as Country Pork with Onions. Mediterranean winters can be as cold and fierce as the summers are hot, so comforting casseroles are also called for. When you need a one-pot dinner to take the chill off a gray winter day, try Traditional Provençal Daube, Moroccan Chicken Couscous, or Basque Pork & Beans.

Traditional Provençal Daube

It isn't sunny all year round in the Mediterranean. In the winter, when the fierce wind, le mistral, *blows through the region, warming hearty stews are served in homes and restaurants.*

Serves 4–6

INGREDIENTS

1 lb. 9 oz. boneless lean stewing
    beef, such as leg, cut into
    2-inch pieces
1²/₃ cups full-bodied dry red wine
2 tbsp. olive oil
4 large garlic cloves, crushed
4 shallots, thinly sliced
9 oz. unsmoked bacon

5–6 tbsp. all-purpose flour
9 oz. large chestnut mushrooms,
    sliced
14 oz. can chopped tomatoes
1 large bouquet garni of 1 bay leaf,
    2 sprigs dried thyme and 2 sprigs
    fresh parsley, tied in a 3-inch piece
    of celery

2-inch strip dried orange rind (see
    page 176) (optional)
2 cups beef stock
1³/₄ oz. can anchovy fillets in oil
2 tbsp. capers in brine, drained
2 tbsp. red wine vinegar
2 tbsp. finely chopped fresh parsley
salt and pepper

1 Place the stewing beef in a non-metallic bowl with the wine, olive oil, half the garlic and the shallots. Cover and marinate for at least 4 hours, stirring occasionally.

2 Meanwhile, place the bacon in a pan of water, bring to a boil, and simmer for 10 minutes. Drain.

3 Place 4 tablespoons of the flour in a bowl and stir in about 2 tablespoons water to make a thick paste. Cover and set aside.

4 Strain the marinated beef, reserving the marinade. Pat the beef dry and toss in seasoned flour.

5 Arrange a layer of bacon, mushrooms, and tomatoes in a large flameproof casserole, then add a layer of beef. Continue

layering until all the ingredients are used, tucking in the bouquet garni and orange rind, if using.

6 Pour in the beef stock and reserved marinade. Spread the flour paste around the rim of the casserole. Press on the lid to make a tight seal (make more paste if necessary).

7 Cook in a preheated oven at 325°F for 2½ hours. Meanwhile, drain the anchovies, then mash with the capers and remaining garlic.

8 Remove the casserole, break the seal and stir in the mashed anchovies, vinegar, and parsley. Re-cover and continue cooking for 1–1½ hours until the meat is tender. Adjust the seasoning and serve.

Vitello Tonnato

This classic dish of cold, thinly sliced veal with a creamy tuna sauce makes the most luxurious hot-weather meal. Serve it chilled with a simple salad accompaniment and a crisp white wine.

Serves 6–8

INGREDIENTS

1 boned and rolled piece of veal leg, about 2 lb. boned weight
olive oil
salt and pepper

TUNA MAYONNAISE:
5½ oz. can tuna in olive oil
2 large eggs*
about 3 tbsp. lemon juice
olive oil

TO GARNISH:
8 black olives, pitted and halved
1 tbsp. capers in brine, rinsed and drained
finely chopped fresh flat-leaf parsley
lemon wedges

*Use pasteurized egg products, available where eggs are sold, to minimize the risk of salmonella.

1 Rub the veal all over with oil and pepper and place in a roasting pan. Cover the pan with a piece of aluminum foil if there isn't any fat on the meat, then roast in a preheated oven at 450°F for 10 minutes. Lower the heat to 350°F and continue roasting for 1 hour for medium, or 1¼ hours if you prefer your veal well done. Set the veal aside and let cool completely, reserving any juices in the roasting pan.

2 Meanwhile, drain the tuna, reserving the oil. Blend the eggs in a food processor with 1 teaspoon of the lemon juice and a pinch of salt. Add enough olive oil to the tuna oil to make up to 1¼ cups.

3 With the motor running, add the oil to the eggs, drop by drop, until a thin mayonnaise forms. Add the tuna and process until smooth. Blend in lemon juice to taste. Adjust the seasoning.

4 Slice the cool meat very thinly. Add any juices to the reserved pan juices. Gradually pour the veal juices into the tuna mayonnaise, whisking until it is a thin, pouring consistency.

5 Layer the veal slices with the sauce on a platter, ending with a layer of sauce. Cover and chill overnight. Garnish with olives, capers, and a light sprinkling of parsley. Arrange lemon wedges around the edge and serve.

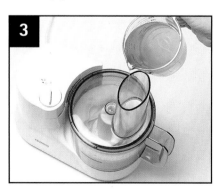

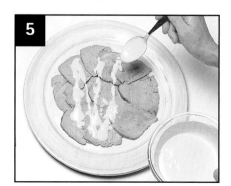

Veal Chops with Salsa Verde

*This vibrant green Italian sauce adds a touch of
Mediterranean flavor to any simply cooked meat or seafood.*

Serves 4

INGREDIENTS

4 veal chops, such as loin chops, about
   8 oz. each and ¾-inch thick
garlic-flavored olive oil, for brushing
salt and pepper
fresh basil or oregano leaves, to garnish

SALSA VERDE:
2 oz. fresh flat-leaf parsley leaves
3 canned anchovy fillets in oil, drained
½ tbsp. capers in brine, rinsed and
   drained
1 shallot, finely chopped

1 garlic clove, halved, green core
   removed and chopped
1 tbsp. lemon juice, or to taste
6 large fresh basil leaves, or ¾ tsp.
   freeze-dried
2 sprigs fresh oregano, or ½ tsp. dried
½ cup extra-virgin olive oil

1 To make the salsa verde, put all the ingredients, except the olive oil, in a blender or food processor and process until they are chopped and blended.

2 With the motor running, add the oil through the top or feed tube and quickly blend until thickened. Add pepper to taste. Transfer to a bowl, cover, and chill.

3 Lightly brush the veal chops with olive oil and season them with salt and pepper. Place under a preheated broiler and cook for about 3 minutes. Turn over, brush with more oil, and broil for a further 2 minutes until cooked when tested with the tip of a knife.

4 Transfer the chops to individual plates and spoon a little of the chilled salsa verde beside them. Garnish the chops with fresh oregano or basil and serve with the remaining salsa verde, passed separately.

COOK'S TIP

The salsa verde will keep for up to 2 days in a covered container in the refrigerator. It is also fantastic served with broiled red mullet. Or use it to replace the pesto sauce in Mediterranean Monkfish (see page 108).

Osso Bucco with Citrus Rinds

Popular throughout all of Italy, you'll also find slow-cooked veal shins in many restaurants along the Mediterranean. The orange and lemon rinds, along with fresh basil, give the dish a real southern Italian flavor.

Serves 6

INGREDIENTS

1–2 tbsp. all-purpose flour
6 meaty slices osso bucco (veal shins)
2 lb. 4 oz. fresh tomatoes, skinned, deseeded, and diced, or 2 14 oz. cans chopped tomatoes
1–2 tbsp. olive oil

9 oz. onions, very finely chopped
9 oz. carrots, finely diced
8 fl oz./1 cup dry white wine
8 fl oz./1 cup veal stock
6 large basil leaves, torn

1 large garlic clove, very finely chopped
finely grated rind of 1 large lemon
finely grated rind of 1 orange
2 tbsp. finely chopped fresh flat-leaf parsley
salt and pepper

1 Put the flour in a plastic bag and season with salt and pepper. Add the osso bucco, a couple of pieces at a time, and shake until well coated. Remove and shake off the excess flour. Continue until all the pieces are coated.

2 If using canned tomatoes, put them in a strainer and let them drain.

3 Heat 1 tablespoon of the oil in a large flameproof casserole.

Add the osso bucco and fry for 10 minutes on each side until well browned. Remove from the pan.

4 Add 1–2 teaspoons oil to the casserole if necessary. Add the onions and fry for about 5 minutes, stirring, until soft. Stir in the carrots and continue frying until they become soft.

5 Add the tomatoes, wine, stock, and basil and return the osso bucco to the pan. Bring to a

boil, then lower the heat and simmer for 1 hour, covered. Check that the meat is tender with the tip of a knife. If not, continue cooking for 10 minutes and test again.

6 When the meat is tender, sprinkle with the garlic and lemon and orange rinds, re-cover and cook for a further 10 minutes.

7 Adjust the seasoning if necessary. Sprinkle with the parsley and serve.

Spanish Chicken with Garlic

The slow cooking takes all the harsh flavoring out of the garlic cloves and makes them meltingly tender in this simple dish.

Serves 4

INGREDIENTS

2–3 tbsp. all-purpose flour
cayenne pepper
4 chicken quarters or other joints,
   patted dry

about 4 tbsp. olive oil
20 large garlic cloves, each halved
   and green core removed
1 large bay leaf

2 cups chicken stock
4 tbsp. dry white wine
chopped fresh parsley, to garnish
salt and pepper

1 Put about 2 tablespoons of the flour in a bag and season to taste with cayenne pepper and salt and pepper. Add a chicken piece and shake until it is lightly coated with the flour, shaking off the excess. Repeat with the remaining pieces, adding more flour and seasoning, if necessary.

2 Heat 3 tablespoons of the olive oil in a large skillet. Add the garlic cloves and fry for about 2 minutes, stirring, to flavor the oil. Remove with a slotted spoon and set aside.

3 Add the chicken pieces to the pan, skin-side down, and fry for 5 minutes, or until the skin is golden brown. Turn and fry for a further 5 minutes, adding an extra 1–2 tablespoons oil if necessary.

4 Return the garlic to the pan. Add the bay leaf, chicken stock, and wine and bring to a boil. Lower the heat, cover, and simmer for 25 minutes, or until the chicken is tender and the garlic cloves are very soft.

5 Using a slotted spoon, transfer the chicken to a serving platter and keep warm. Bring the cooking liquid to a boil, with the garlic, and boil until reduced to about 1 cup plus 2 tbsp.. Adjust the seasoning, if necessary.

6 Spoon the sauce over the chicken pieces and scatter the garlic cloves around. Garnish with parsley and serve.

COOK'S TIP

The cooked garlic cloves are delicious mashed into a puree on the side of the plate for smearing on the chicken pieces.

Moroccan Chicken Couscous

'Couscous' is the name of both the small grains that are a staple of Moroccan kitchens and the fragrant, spicy meat or vegetable stew traditionally served with it.

Serves 4–6

INGREDIENTS

about 3 tbsp. olive oil

8 chicken pieces with bones, such as quarters, breasts, and legs

2 large onions, chopped

2 large garlic cloves, crushed

1-inch piece fresh root ginger, peeled and finely chopped

5 ½ oz. dried chickpeas, soaked overnight and drained

4 large carrots, cut into thick chunks

large pinch of saffron threads, dissolved in 2 tbsp. boiling water

finely grated rind of 2 lemons

2 red bell peppers, cored, deseeded and sliced

2 large zucchini, cut into chunks

2 tomatoes, cored, deseeded, and chopped

3½ oz. dried apricots, chopped

½ tsp. ground cumin

½ tsp. ground coriander

½ tsp. cayenne pepper, or to taste

2 ½ cups water

1 tbsp. butter

3⅓ cups instant couscous

salt and pepper

harissa, to serve (optional)

1 Heat 3 tablespoons of the oil in a large flameproof casserole. Pat the chicken pieces dry with paper towels, add to the oil, skin-side down, and cook for 5 minutes until crisp and brown. Remove from the pan and set aside.

2 Add the onions to the pan, adding a little extra oil, if necessary. Fry the onions for 5 minutes, then add the garlic and ginger and fry for a further 2 minutes, stirring occasionally.

3 Return the chicken pieces to the casserole. Add the chickpeas, carrots, saffron, and lemon rind. Pour in enough water to cover by 1 inch and bring to a boil.

4 Lower the heat, cover, and simmer for 45 minutes, or until the chickpeas are tender. Add the peppers, zucchini, tomatoes, dried apricots, cumin, coriander, cayenne pepper, and salt and pepper to taste. Re-cover and simmer for a further 15 minutes.

5 Meanwhile, bring the water to a boil. Stir in ½ teaspoon salt and the butter. Sprinkle in the couscous. Cover the pan tightly, remove from the heat and let it stand for 10 minutes, or until the grains are tender.

6 Fluff the couscous with a fork. Taste and adjust the seasoning of the stew. Spoon the couscous into individual bowls and serve the stew and a bowl of harissa, if using, separately.

Provençal Barbecued Lamb

Be generous with the fresh herbs and the aromas will transport you to the Provençal countryside! Ratatouille (see page 134) is the ideal accompaniment.

Serves 4–6

INGREDIENTS

1 leg of lamb, about 3 lbs. 5 oz., boned
about 1 quantity Black Olive Tapenade
   (see page 16)
olive oil, for brushing
fresh rosemary and thyme sprigs, to

garnish

MARINADE:
1 bottle full-bodied red wine
2 large garlic cloves, chopped

2 tbsp. extra-virgin olive oil
large handful fresh rosemary sprigs
fresh thyme sprigs

1 Place the boned lamb on a chopping board. Holding the knife almost flat, slice horizontally into the pocket left by the leg bone, taking care not to cut all the way through, so the boned meat can be opened out flat, like a book.

2 Place the lamb in a large non-metallic bowl and add all the marinade ingredients. Cover with plastic wrap and marinate for at least 6 hours, but preferably up to 24 hours, turning the meat over several times.

3 When ready to cook, remove the lamb from the marinade and pat dry. Lay the lamb flat and thread 2 or 3 long metal skewers through the flesh, so that the meat remains flat while it cooks. Spread the tapenade all over the lamb on both sides.

4 Brush the barbecue rack with oil. Place the lamb on the rack about 4 inches above hot coals and cook for 5 minutes. Turn the meat over, and continue cooking for about 5 minutes longer. Turn twice more at 5 minute intervals,

brushing with extra tapenade. Raise the rack to 6 inches if the meat starts to look charred—it should be medium cooked after 20–25 minutes.

5 Remove the lamb from the heat and let it rest for 10 minutes before carving into thin slices and serving, garnished with rosemary and thyme sprigs.

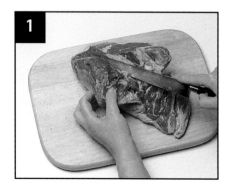

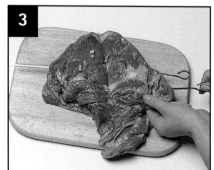

Lamb Skewers on Rosemary

*Wild rosemary scents the air all over the Mediterranean – here, branches
of the herb are used as skewers for succulent lamb cubes with Turkish flavorings.*

Makes 4

INGREDIENTS

1 lb. 2 oz. boneless leg of lamb
4 long, thick branches fresh rosemary
1 or 2 red bell peppers, depending
   on the size

12 large garlic cloves, peeled
olive oil
Spiced Pilau with Saffron
   (see page 196), to serve

MARINADE:
2 tbsp. olive oil
2 tbsp. dry white wine
1/2 tsp. ground cumin
1 sprig fresh oregano, chopped

1 At least 4 hours before cooking, cut the lamb into 2-inch cubes. Mix all the marinade ingredients together in a bowl. Add the lamb cubes, stir well to coat, and marinate for at least 4 hours, or up to 12 hours.

2 An hour before cooking, put the rosemary in a bowl of cold water and let soak.

3 Slice the tops off the bell peppers, cut the bell peppers in half, quarter, and remove the cores and seeds. Cut the halves into 2-inch pieces.

4 Bring a small saucepan of water to a boil, blanch the pepper pieces and garlic cloves for 1 minute. Drain and refresh under cold water. Pat dry and set aside.

5 Remove the rosemary from the water and pat dry. To make the skewers, remove the rosemary needles from about the first 1¾ inches of the branches so you have a "handle" to turn them over with while broiling.

6 Thread alternate pieces of lamb, garlic, and red pepper pieces on to the 4 rosemary skewers; the meat should be tender enough to push the sprig through it, but, if not, use a metal skewer to poke a hole in the center of each cube.

7 Lightly oil the broiler rack. Place the skewers on the rack about 5 inches under a preheated hot broiler and broil for 10–12 minutes, brushing with any leftover marinade or olive oil and turning, until the meat is cooked. Serve with the pilau.

Cypriot Lamb with Orzo

This old-fashioned recipe, which uses an inexpensive cut of lamb, fits the bill when you are catering for a crowd because it requires very little attention while cooking—you can leave it alone for 4 hours!

Serves 6

INGREDIENTS

2 large garlic cloves	4 sprigs fresh thyme	9 oz. orzo pasta (see
1 unboned shoulder of lamb	4 sprigs fresh parsley	Cook's Tip)
2 x 14 oz. cans chopped	1 bay leaf	salt and pepper
tomatoes	½ cup water	fresh thyme sprigs, to garnish

1 Cut the garlic cloves in half and remove the green cores, then thinly slice. Using the tip of a sharp knife, make slits all over the lamb shoulder, then insert the garlic slices into the slits.

2 Pour the tomatoes and their juices into a roasting pan large enough to hold the lamb shoulder. Add the thyme, parsley, and bay leaf. Place the lamb on top, skin-side up, and cover the dish tightly with a sheet of foil, shiny side down. Scrunch the foil all around the edge so that none of the juices escape during cooking.

3 Put in a preheated oven at 325°F and cook for 3 ½–4 hours until the lamb is tender and the tomatoes are reduced to a thick sauce.

4 Remove the lamb from the roasting pan and set aside. Using a large metal spoon, skim off as much fat from the surface of the tomato sauce as possible.

5 Add the water and orzo to the tomatoes, stirring so the grains are submerged. Add a little extra water if the sauce seems too thick. Season to taste with salt and pepper. Return the lamb to the roasting pan.

6 Re-cover the roasting pan and return to the oven for 15 minutes, or until the orzo is tender. Remove the bay leaf. Let the lamb rest for 10 minutes, then slice and serve with the orzo in tomato juice, garnished with fresh thyme sprigs.

COOK'S TIP

Orzo is a small pasta shape that looks like barley grains.

Basque Pork & Beans

Dried cannellini beans feature in many Italian, Spanish, French, and Greek stews and casseroles, especially during the winter. The sweet bell peppers and orange add a Spanish Mediterranean flavor.

Serves 4–6

INGREDIENTS

7 oz. dried cannellini beans, soaked
   overnight
olive oil
1 lb. 4 oz. boneless leg of pork, cut
   into 2-inch chunks

1 large onion, sliced
3 large garlic cloves, crushed
14 oz. can chopped tomatoes
2 green bell peppers, cored,
   deseeded, and sliced

finely grated rind of 1 large orange
salt and pepper
finely chopped fresh parsley, to garnish

1 Drain the cannellini beans and put in a large saucepan with fresh water to cover. Bring to a boil and boil rapidly for 10 minutes. Lower the heat and simmer for 20 minutes. Drain and set aside.

2 Add enough oil to cover the base of a skillet in a very thin layer. Heat the oil over medium heat, add a few pieces of the pork, and fry on all sides until brown. Repeat with the remaining pork and set aside.

3 Add 1 tablespoon oil to the skillet, if necessary, then add the onion and fry for 3 minutes. Stir in the garlic and fry for a further 2 minutes. Return the pork to the pan.

4 Add the tomatoes to the pan and bring to a boil. Lower the heat, stir in the bell pepper slices, orange rind, the drained beans, and salt and pepper to taste.

5 Transfer the contents of the pan to a casserole.

6 Cover the casserole and cook in a preheated oven at 350°F for 45 minutes, until the beans and pork are tender. Sprinkle with parsley and serve.

VARIATIONS

Any leftover beans and bell peppers can be used as a pasta sauce. Add sliced and fried chorizo sausage for a spicier dish.

Country Pork with Onions

Wherever there are pigs in the Mediterranean, you'll find rustic stews like this, making the most of inexpensive cuts that require slow cooking and robust flavoring.

Serves 4

INGREDIENTS

2 large pork shanks
2 large garlic cloves, sliced
3 tbsp. olive oil
2 carrots, finely chopped
2 celery ribs, strings removed and
  finely chopped

1 large onion, finely chopped
2 sprigs fresh thyme, broken into
  pieces
2 sprigs fresh rosemary, broken into
  pieces
1 large bay leaf

1 cup dry white wine
1 cup water
20 pickling onions
salt and pepper
roughly chopped fresh flat-leaf
  parsley, to garnish

1 Using the tip of a sharp knife, make slits all over the pork shanks and insert the garlic slices.

2 Heat 1 tablespoon of the oil in a flameproof casserole over medium heat. Add the carrots, celery, and onion and fry, stirring occasionally, for about 10 minutes.

3 Place the pork shanks on top of the vegetables. Scatter the thyme and rosemary over the meat. Add the bay leaf, wine, and water, and season with pepper.

4 Bring to a boil, then remove from the heat. Cover tightly and cook in a preheated oven at 325°F for 3 ½ hours, or until the meat is very tender.

5 Meanwhile, put the onions in a bowl, pour boiling water over them, and leave for 1 minute. Drain, then slip off all the skins. Heat the remaining oil in a large skillet. Add the onions, partially cover, and cook over low heat for 15 minutes, shaking the pan occasionally, until the

onions are just starting to turn golden.

6 When the pork shanks are tender, add the onions and continue to cook in the oven for a further 15 minutes for the onions to become tender. Remove the pork and onions and keep warm.

7 Using a large metal spoon, skim off as much fat as possible from the surface of the cooking liquid. Strain the cooking liquid into a bowl, pressing down lightly to extract the flavor; reserve the strained vegetables in the strainer. Adjust the seasoning.

8 Cut the meat from the pork shanks, if desired, then arrange on a serving platter with the onions and strained vegetables. Spoon the sauce over the meat and vegetables. Garnish with parsley.

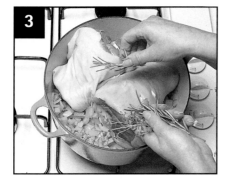

Maltese Rabbit with Fennel

Rabbit is a popular ingredient on the small Mediterranean island of Malta. There are even restaurants where it features as the house specialty, rather than seafood as one might expect.

Serves 4

INGREDIENTS

5 tbsp. olive oil
2 large fennel bulbs, trimmed and
   sliced
2 carrots, diced
1 large garlic clove, crushed
1 tbsp. fennel seeds
about 4 tbsp. all-purpose flour

2 wild rabbits, jointed
1 cup dry white wine
1 cup water
1 bouquet garni of 2 sprigs fresh
   flat-leaf parsley, 1 sprig fresh
   rosemary and 1 bay leaf, tied in a
   3-inch piece of celery

salt and pepper
thick, crusty bread, to serve

TO GARNISH:
finely chopped fresh flat-leaf parsley
   or cilantro
fresh rosemary sprigs

1 Heat 3 tablespoons of the olive oil over medium heat in a large flameproof casserole. Add the fennel and carrots and cook for 5 minutes, stirring occasionally. Stir in the garlic and fennel seeds and continue to cook for 2 minutes, or until the fennel is tender. Remove the fennel and carrots from the casserole and set aside.

2 Put 4 tablespoons flour in a plastic bag and season. Add 2 rabbit pieces and shake to lightly coat, then shake off any excess flour. Continue until all the pieces of rabbit are coated, adding more flour, if necessary.

3 Add the remaining oil to the casserole. Fry the rabbit pieces for about 5 minutes on each side until golden brown, working in batches. Remove the rabbit from the casserole as it is cooked.

4 Pour in the wine and simmer over heat, stirring to scrape up all the bits from the bottom. Return the rabbit pieces, fennel, and carrots to the casserole and pour in the water. Add the bouquet garni and salt and pepper to taste.

5 Bring to a boil. Lower the heat, cover, and simmer for about 1¼ hours until the rabbit is tender.

6 Discard the bouquet garni. Garnish with herbs and serve straight from the casserole with lots of bread to mop up the juices.

Pickled Tuna

When Mediterranean fishermen bring in a bountiful day's catch,
some of the fish is traditionally preserved so that it can be enjoyed a few days later.

Serves 4

INGREDIENTS

4 large tuna steaks, each about
  8 oz. and ³/₄ inch thick
1 cup olive oil
2 large red onions, thinly sliced
2 carrots, thinly sliced
2 large bay leaves, torn

1 garlic clove, very finely chopped
1 cup white wine vinegar or sherry
  vinegar
¹/₂ tsp. dried chili flakes, or to taste,
  crushed
1 tbsp. coriander seeds, lightly crushed

salt and pepper
finely chopped fresh parsley, to garnish

1 Rinse and pat the tuna steaks dry with paper towels. Heat 4 tablespoons of the oil in a large skillet, preferably non-stick.

2 Add the tuna steaks to the pan and fry for 2 minutes over medium–high heat. Turn the steaks and continue to cook for 2 minutes, until browned and medium cooked, or 4 minutes for well done. Remove the tuna from the pan and drain well on paper towels. Set aside.

3 Heat the remaining oil in the pan. Add the onions and cook for 8 minutes, stirring frequently, until soft but not brown. Stir in the carrots, bay leaves, garlic, vinegar, dried chilies, and salt and pepper to taste and continue cooking for 10 minutes, or until the carrots are tender. Stir in the coriander seeds 1 minute before the end of the cooking time.

4 When the tuna steaks are cool enough to be handled easily, remove any skin and bones from

them. Break each of the steaks into 4 or 5 large chunks.

5 Put the fish pieces in a non-metallic bowl and pour the hot onion mixture over them. Very gently mix together, taking care not to break up the fish pieces.

6 Leave until completely cool, then cover and chill for at least 24 hours. The fish will stay fresh in the refrigerator for up to 5 days. To serve, sprinkle with parsley and serve at room temperature.

Seared Tuna with Anchovy & Orange Butter

Meaty tuna steaks have enough flavor to stand up to the robust taste of anchovies.
Serve this with pan-fried potatoes or a mixed rice dish.

Serves 4

INGREDIENTS

olive oil
4 thick tuna steaks, each about
   8 oz. and ¾ inch thick

ANCHOVY AND ORANGE BUTTER:
8 anchovy fillets in oil, drained
4 scallions, finely chopped
1 tbsp. finely grated orange rind
8 tbsp. unsalted butter

¼ tsp. lemon juice
pepper

TO GARNISH:
fresh flat-leaf parsley sprigs
orange rind strips

1 To make the anchovy and orange butter, very finely chop the anchovies and put them in a bowl with the scallions, orange rind, and softened butter. Beat until all the ingredients are blended together, seasoning with lemon juice and pepper to taste.

2 Place the flavored butter on a sheet of waxed paper and roll up into a log shape. Fold over the ends and place in the freezer for 15 minutes to become firm.

3 To cook the tuna, heat a ridged skillet over high heat. Lightly brush the pan with olive oil, add the tuna steaks, in batches if necessary, and fry for 2 minutes. Turn the steaks over and fry for 2 minutes for rare, or up to 4 minutes for well done. Season to taste with salt and pepper.

4 Transfer to a warm plate and put 2 thin slices of anchovy butter on each tuna steak. Garnish with parsley sprigs and orange rind and serve at once.

VARIATION

If you particularly like hot, spicy food, add a pinch of dried chili flakes to the butter mixture.

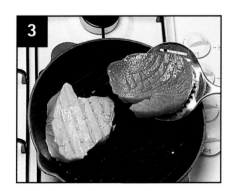

Mediterranean Fish Soup

No trip to the Mediterranean is complete without a steaming bowl of fish soup at a harbor-side restaurant. This simple version is similar to the ones you can enjoy along the Provençal coast.

Serves 4

INGREDIENTS

2 lb. 4 oz. mixed fish, such as sea bass, skate, red snapper, rock fish, and any Mediterranean fish you can find
2 tbsp. olive oil
1 bulb fennel, trimmed and chopped
2 shallots, chopped
2 garlic cloves, chopped
1 lb. 4 oz. sun-ripened tomatoes, chopped

1 bouquet garni of 2 sprigs fresh flat-leaf parsley, 2 sprigs fresh thyme and 1 bay leaf, tied in a 3-inch piece of celery
pinch of saffron threads
3 cups Mediterranean Fish Stock (see page 180), or good-quality, ready-made chilled fish stock
salt and pepper

French pastis or other aniseed-flavored liqueur (optional)

TO SERVE:
Rouille (see page 186)
1 loaf French bread, sliced and toasted
4½ oz. Gruyère cheese, grated

1 To prepare the fish, remove any skin and bones and chop.

2 Heat the oil in a heavy-based pan. Add the fennel and cook for 5 minutes, stirring frequently. Add the shallots and garlic and cook for about 5 minutes until the fennel is tender.

3 Stir in the mixed fish and add the tomatoes, bouquet garni, saffron, fish stock, and salt and pepper to taste.

4 Slowly bring almost to a boil, stirring occasionally. Lower the heat, partially cover, and simmer for 30 minutes, stirring occasionally to break up the tomatoes. Skim the surface as necessary.

5 Remove the bouquet garni. Process the soup in a food processor, then work it through a food mill into a large bowl.

6 Return to the rinsed-out pan and heat without boiling. Adjust the seasoning. Stir in a little pastis, if using.

7 Spread the rouille on the toast and top with the cheese. Place in each bowl and ladle the hot soup over the toast. Serve at once.

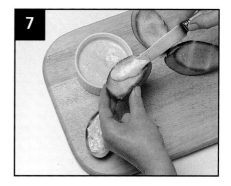

Seafood Stew

Similar to Bouillabaisse, the traditional French stew, this "meal in a pot" should contain the best of the day's offering at your fish market. The seafood is expensive, so it is important to use a good fish stock.

Serves 4–6

INGREDIENTS

8 oz. clams

1 lb. 9 oz. mixed fish, such as sea bass, skate, red snapper, rock fish, and any Mediterranean fish you can find

12–18 tiger shrimp

about 3 tbsp. olive oil

1 large onion, finely chopped

2 garlic cloves, very finely chopped

2 sun-ripened tomatoes, halved, deseeded, and chopped

3 cups Mediterranean Fish Stock (see page 180), or good-quality, ready-made chilled fish stock

1 tbsp. tomato paste

1 tsp. fresh thyme leaves

pinch of saffron threads

pinch of sugar

salt and pepper

finely chopped fresh parsley, to garnish

1 Soak the clams in a bowl of lightly salted water for 30 minutes. Rinse them under cold, running water and lightly scrub to remove any sand from the shells. Discard any broken clams or open clams that do not shut when firmly tapped with the back of a knife, as these will be unsafe to eat.

2 Prepare the fish as necessary, removing any skin and bones, then cut into bite-sized chunks.

3 To prepare the shrimp, break off the heads. Peel off the shells, leaving the tails intact, if desired. Using a small knife, make a slit along the back of each and remove the thin black vein. Set all the seafood aside.

4 Heat the oil in a large pan. Add the onion and fry for 5 minutes, stirring. Add the garlic and fry for about another 2 minutes until the onion is soft, but not brown.

5 Add the tomatoes, stock, tomato paste, thyme leaves, saffron threads, and sugar, then bring to a boil, stirring to dissolve the tomato paste. Lower the heat, cover, and simmer for 15 minutes. Adjust the seasoning.

6 Add the seafood and simmer until the clams open and the fish flakes easily. Discard the bouquet garni and any clams that do not open. Garnish and serve at once.

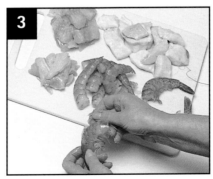

Salt Cod Fritters

Mediterranean cooks have always made the most of dried salted cod, once the only source of cod during harsh winter months. These fritters come from the south of France.

Serves 6

INGREDIENTS

1 lb. salt cod
12 oz. floury baking potatoes
1 tbsp. olive oil, plus extra for frying
1 onion, very finely chopped

1 garlic clove, crushed
4 tbsp. very finely chopped fresh
  parsley or cilantro
1 tbsp. capers in brine, drained and

finely chopped (optional)
1 small egg, lightly beaten
salt and pepper
Aioli (see page 184), to serve

1 Break the salt cod into pieces and place in a bowl. Add enough water to cover and leave for 48 hours, changing the water 4 times.

2 Drain the salt cod, then cook in boiling water for 20–25 minutes until tender. Drain, then remove all the skin and bones. Using a fork, flake the fish into fine pieces that still retain some texture.

3 Meanwhile, boil the potatoes in their skins until tender. Drain, peel, and mash in a large bowl. Set aside.

4 Heat 1 tablespoon of the oil in a skillet. Add the onion and garlic and fry for 5 minutes, stirring, until tender but not brown. Remove with a slotted spoon and drain on paper towels.

5 Stir the salt cod, onion, and garlic into the mashed potatoes. Stir in the parsley and capers, if using. Season generously with pepper.

6 Stir in the beaten egg. Cover and chill for 30 minutes, then adjust the seasoning.

7 Heat 2 inches oil in a skillet to 350–375°F, or until a cube of bread browns in 30 seconds. Drop tablespoonfuls of the salt-cod mixture into the hot oil and fry for about 8 minutes, or until golden brown and set. Do not fry more than 6 at a time because the oil will become too cold and the fritters will become soggy. You will get 18–20 fritters.

8 Drain the fritters on paper towels. Serve at once with aioli for dipping. Garnish with parsley.

Shrimp Skewers with Tomato Salsa

Shrimp of all sizes are popular fare in the Mediterranean, where they are often cooked very simply by broiling—the key is not to overcook them.

Makes 8 skewers

INGREDIENTS

32 large tiger shrimp
olive oil, for brushing
skordalia (see page 188) or aioli (see page 184), to serve

MARINADE
½ cup extra-virgin olive oil
2 tbsp. lemon juice

1 tsp. finely chopped red chili
1 tsp. balsamic vinegar
pepper

TOMATO SALSA:
2 large sun-ripened tomatoes, skinned, cored, deseeded, and chopped
4 scallions, white parts only, very finely chopped

1 red bell pepper, skinned, deseeded, and chopped
1 orange or yellow bell pepper, skinned, deseeded, and chopped
1 tbsp. extra-virgin olive oil
2 tsp. balsamic vinegar
4 sprigs fresh basil

1 To make the marinade, place all the ingredients in a non-metallic bowl and whisk together. Set aside.

2 To prepare the shrimp, break off the heads. Peel off the shells, leaving the tails intact. Using a small knife, make a slit along the back and remove the thin black vein. Add the shrimp to the marinade and stir until well coated. Cover and chill for 15 minutes.

3 Make the salsa. Put all the ingredients, except the basil, in a non-metallic bowl and toss together. Season to taste with salt and pepper.

4 Thread 4 shrimp onto a metal skewer, bending each in half. Repeat with 7 more skewers. Brush with marinade.

5 Brush a broiler rack with oil. Place the skewers on the rack, then position under a preheated hot broiler, about 3 inches from the heat; cook for 1 minute. Turn the skewers over, brush again and continue to cook for 1–1½ minutes until the shrimp turn pink and opaque.

6 Tear the basil leaves and toss with the salsa. Arrange each skewer on a plate with some salsa and garnish with parsley. Serve with skordalia or aioli dip.

Swordfish à la Maltese

The firm texture of swordfish means it is often simply grilled, but it also lends itself to this delicate technique of cooking in a paper parcel. When you open the paper, the unmistakable Mediterranean aromas waft out.

Makes 4

INGREDIENTS

1 tbsp. fennel seeds
2 tbsp. fruity extra-virgin olive oil, plus extra for brushing and drizzling
2 large onions, thinly sliced

1 small garlic clove, crushed
4 swordfish steaks, about 6 oz. each
1 large lemon, cut in half

2 large sun-ripened tomatoes, finely chopped
4 sprigs fresh thyme
salt and pepper

1 Place the fennel seeds in a dry skillet over medium-high heat and toast, stirring, until they give off their aroma, watching carefully so that they do not burn. Immediately pour out of the pan onto a plate. Set aside.

2 Heat 2 tablespoons of the olive oil in the pan. Add the onions and fry for 5 minutes, stirring occasionally. Add the garlic and continue frying the onions until very soft and tender, but not brown. Remove the pan from the heat.

3 Cut out four 12-inch circles of baking parchment. Very lightly brush the center of each paper circle with olive oil. Equally divide the onions between the paper circles, flattening them out to about the size of the fish steaks.

4 Top the onions in each parcel with a swordfish steak. Squeeze lemon juice over the fish steaks and drizzle with a little olive oil. Scatter the tomatoes over the top, add a sprig of thyme to each, and season with salt and pepper to taste.

5 Fold the edges of the paper together, scrunching them tightly so no cooking juices escape during cooking. Place on a cookie sheet and cook in a preheated oven at 400°F for 20 minutes.

6 To test if the fish is cooked, open one package and pierce the flesh with a knife—it should flake easily. Serve straight from the paper packages.

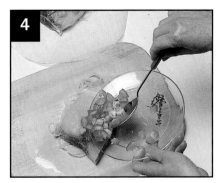

Mediterranean Monkfish

As any Mediterranean cook will tell you, some of the best seafood dishes are the simplest, and this recipe proves the point. It's ideal for serving in hot weather, when you want to spend as little time as possible in the kitchen.

Serves 4

INGREDIENTS

1 lb. 4 oz. vine-ripened cherry tomatoes, a mixture of yellow and red, if available

2 monkfish fillets, about 12 oz. each
8 tbsp. Pesto Sauce (see page 124)

salt and pepper
fresh basil sprigs, to garnish

1 Cut the tomatoes in half and scatter, cut-sides up, on the base of an ovenproof serving dish. Set aside.

2 Using your fingers, rub off the thin gray membrane that covers monkfish.

3 If the skin has not been removed, place the fish skin-side down on the work surface. Loosen enough skin at one end of the fillet so you can grip hold of it. Work from the front of the fillet to the back. Insert the knife, almost flat, and using a gentle sawing action, remove the skin.

Rinse the fillets well and dry with paper towels.

4 Place the fillets on top of the tomatoes, tucking the thin end under, if necessary (see Cook's Tip). Spread 4 tablespoons of the pesto sauce over each fillet and season with pepper.

5 Cover the dish tightly with foil, shiny-side down. Place in a preheated oven at 450°F and roast for 16–18 minutes until the fish is cooked through, the flesh flakes easily, and the tomatoes are dissolving into a thick sauce.

6 Adjust the seasoning, if necessary. Garnish with basil sprigs and serve at once with new potatoes.

COOK'S TIP

Monkfish fillets are often cut from the tail, which means one end is much thinner than the rest and prone to overcooking. If you can't get fillets that are the same thickness, fold the thin end under for even cooking.

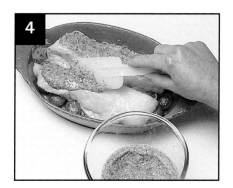

Wrapped Red Mullet with Stewed Bell Peppers & Fennel

Fresh thyme, which grows wild throughout the Mediterranean, flavors this rustic dish. Serve with boiled new potatoes.

Serves 4

INGREDIENTS

3 tbsp. olive oil, plus extra for rubbing

2 large red bell peppers, cored, deseeded, and thinly sliced

2 large bulbs fennel, trimmed and thinly sliced

1 large clove garlic, crushed

8 sprigs fresh thyme, plus extra for garnishing

20–24 grape leaves in brine

1 lemon

4 red mullet, about 8 oz. each, scaled and gutted

salt and pepper

1 Heat the oil in a large skillet over medium-low heat. Add the bell peppers, fennel, garlic, and 4 sprigs of thyme and stir together. Cook, stirring occasionally, for about 20 minutes until the vegetables are cooked thoroughly and are very soft, but not browned.

2 Meanwhile, rinse the grape leaves under cold, running water and pat dry with paper towels. Slice 4 thin slices off the lemon,

then cut each slice in half. Finely grate the rind of ½ the lemon.

3 Stuff the mullet cavities with the lemon slices and remaining thyme sprigs. Rub a little olive oil on each fish and sprinkle with the lemon rind. Season with salt and pepper to taste.

4 Wrap 5 or 6 grape leaves around each mullet, depending on the size of the mullet, to completely enclose.

Put the wrapped mullet on top of the fennel and bell peppers. Cover the pan and cook over medium-low heat for 12–15 minutes until the fish is cooked through and the flesh flakes easily when tested with the tip of a knife.

5 Transfer the cooked fish to individual plates and spoon the fennel and bell peppers alongside. Garnish with thyme sprigs and serve.

Moules Marinara

The Spanish, French, and Italians all serve variations of this simple mussel recipe, which is universally popular. Use the freshest mussels you can find and cook them on the day you buy them.

Serves 4

INGREDIENTS

4 lb. 8 oz. live mussels
4 tbsp. olive oil
4–6 large garlic cloves, halved
2 x 14 oz. cans chopped
   tomatoes

1¼ cups dry white wine
2 tbsp. finely chopped fresh flat-leaf
   parsley, plus extra for garnishing
1 tbsp. finely chopped fresh oregano

salt and pepper
French bread, to serve

1 Soak the mussels in a bowl of lightly salted water for 30 minutes. Rinse them under cold, running water and lightly scrub to remove any sand from the shells. Using a small sharp knife, remove the "beards" from the shells.

2 Discard any broken mussels or open mussels that do not shut when firmly tapped with the back of a knife. This indicates that they are dead and could cause food poisoning if eaten. Rinse the mussels again, then set aside in a colander.

3 Heat the olive oil in a large saucepan or stockpot over medium-high heat. Add the garlic and fry, stirring, for about 3 minutes to flavor the oil. Using a slotted spoon, remove the garlic from the pan.

4 Add the tomatoes and their juice, the wine, parsley, and oregano and bring to a boil, stirring. Lower the heat, cover, and simmer for 5 minutes to allow the flavors to blend.

5 Add the mussels, cover the pan, and simmer for 5–8 minutes, shaking the pan regularly, until the mussels open. Using a slotted spoon, transfer the mussels to serving bowls, discarding any that are not open.

6 Season the sauce with salt and pepper to taste. Ladle the sauce over the mussels, sprinkle with extra chopped parsley, and serve at once with plenty of French bread to mop up the delicious juices.

Seared Scallops with Champagne-Saffron Sauce

Coming straight from the finest Riviera restaurants, this rich and extravagant dish is surprisingly simple and only needs plain boiled rice as an accompaniment.

Serves 4

INGREDIENTS

generous pinch of saffron threads
about 4 tbsp. unsalted butter
20 large scallops with the corals, each at least 1 inch thick, shelled, with any juices reserved

4 tbsp. dry champagne or sparkling wine
1¼ cups heavy cream
½ lemon

salt and pepper
fresh flat-leaf parsley sprigs, to garnish

1 Heat a large dry skillet, preferably non-stick, over high heat. Add the saffron threads and toast just until they start to give off their aroma. Immediately pour onto a plate and set aside.

2 Melt half the butter in the pan. Add half the scallops and fry for 2 minutes. Turn and fry for a further 1½–2 minutes until the scallops are set and the flesh is opaque all the way though when you pierce one with a knife (see Cook's Tip).

3 Transfer the scallops to a hot dish, cover, and keep warm while cooking the rest in the same way, adding more butter as necessary.

4 Add the saffron to the cooking juices and pour in the champagne, cream and any reserved scallop juices, stirring. Bring to a boil, then lower the heat slightly and simmer for about 10 minutes until reduced to a consistency that coats the back of a spoon.

5 Add freshly squeezed lemon juice and salt and pepper to taste. Return the scallops to the pan and stir until just heated through. Transfer to 4 plates and garnish with parsley. Serve at once.

COOK'S TIP

The exact cooking time depends on the thickness of the scallops. If the scallops are thinner, only cook them for 1½ minutes on each side. Take great care not to overcook them.

Squid Salad

When you want to avoid the heat of the kitchen on a hot day, prepare this the evening before, put it in the refrigerator, and forget about it until you are ready to serve.

Serves 4–6

INGREDIENTS

2 lb. small squid
½ cup lemon juice
¼ cup extra-virgin olive oil
1 oz. fresh flat-leaf parsley
8 scallions

4 vine-ripened tomatoes, deseeded
  and chopped
salt and pepper

TO GARNISH:
radicchio leaves
finely chopped red chilies (optional)
capers or black olives (optional)
finely chopped fresh flat-leaf parsley

1 To prepare each squid, pull the head and all the insides out of the body sac. Cut the tentacles off the head and discard the head. Remove the beak from the center of the tentacles.

2 Pull out the thin, transparent quill that runs through the center of the body. Rinse the body sac under running cold water and, using your fingers, rub off the thin, gray membrane. Cut the squid body sacs into ½-inch slices. Rinse the tentacle pieces and set aside with the body slices.

3 Put the lemon juice and olive oil in a large bowl and stir together. Very finely chop the parsley and add to the bowl. Finely chop the white parts of the scallions and add to the bowl with the tomatoes. Season with salt and pepper to taste.

4 Bring a pan of lightly salted water to a boil. Add all the squid and return to a boil.

5 As soon as the water returns to a boil, drain the squid. Add the squid to the bowl of dressing

and gently toss all the ingredients together.

6 Let the squid cool completely, then cover and marinate in the refrigerator for at least 6 hours, preferably overnight.

7 Line a serving bowl with radicchio leaves. Add the chopped chili, capers or olives, to taste, if you are using them. Mound the squid salad on top of the radicchio leaves and sprinkle with finely chopped parsley. Serve very chilled.

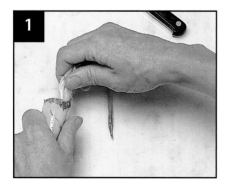

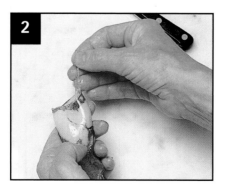

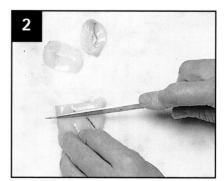

Salade Niçoise

This classic salad from Nice is often made with canned tuna,
but using seared fresh tuna steaks instead gives it a sophisticated twist.

Serves 4–6

INGREDIENTS

3 large eggs
9 oz. French (green) beans, topped
9 oz. small waxy potatoes, such as
  Charlottes, scrubbed and halved
1 large, sun-ripened tomato, cut into
  eighths

1 large tuna steak, about 12 oz. and
  ³/₄ inch thick, seared (see page 96)
¹/₂ cup Provençal-style Olives (see page
  172), or plain black olives
1 ³/₄ oz. can anchovy fillets in oil,
  drained
1 tbsp. chopped fresh flat-leaf parsley

GARLIC VINAIGRETTE:
scant ¹/₂ cup extra-virgin olive oil
3 tbsp. red or white wine vinegar
¹/₂ tsp. sugar
¹/₂ tsp. Dijon mustard
2 garlic cloves, crushed
salt and pepper

1 To make the vinaigrette, put all the ingredients in a screw-top jar and shake until blended. Season with salt and pepper to taste. Set aside.

2 Bring 3 pans of water to a boil. Add the eggs to one pan, bring back to a boil, then cook for 12 minutes. Drain immediately and run under cold running water to stop further cooking.

3 Put the beans and potatoes into separate pans of boiling water. Blanch the beans for 3 minutes, then drain and immediately transfer to a large bowl. Shake the dressing and pour it over the beans.

4 Continue to cook the potatoes until they are tender, then drain and add to the beans and dressing while they are still hot. Allow the potatoes and beans to cool in the dressing.

5 Add the tomato pieces to the vegetables in the dressing and toss together. Break the tuna into large chunks and gently toss with the other ingredients.

6 Shell the hard-boiled eggs and cut each into quarters lengthwise.

7 Mound the tuna and vegetables on a large serving platter. Arrange the hard-boiled egg quarters around the side. Scatter the olives over the salad, then arrange the anchovies in a lattice on top. Cover and chill.

8 About 15 minutes before serving, remove the salad from the refrigerator and allow to come to room temperature. Sprinkle with parsley and serve.

Lobster Salad

*Lobsters are as expensive along the Mediterranean as they are in other parts of the world,
so it is best to prepare them simply to ensure that none of the rich, sweet flavor is lost.*

Serves 2

INGREDIENTS

2 raw lobster tails
salt and pepper

LEMON-DILL MAYONNAISE:
1 large lemon
1 large egg yolk*
$^{1}/_{2}$ tsp. Dijon mustard
$^{2}/_{3}$ cup olive oil
1 tbsp. chopped fresh dill

TO GARNISH:
radicchio leaves
lemon wedges
fresh dill sprigs

*Use pasteurized egg products, available where eggs are sold, to minimize the risk of salmonella.

1 To make the lemon-dill mayonnaise, finely grate the rind from the lemon and squeeze the juice. Beat the egg yolk in a small bowl and beat in the mustard and 1 teaspoon of the lemon juice.

2 Using a balloon whisk or electric mixer, beat in the olive oil, drop by drop, until a thick mayonnaise forms. Stir in half the lemon rind and 1 tablespoon of the juice.

3 Season with salt and pepper, and add more lemon juice if desired. Stir in the dill and cover with plastic wrap. Chill until required.

4 Bring a large saucepan of salted water to a boil. Add the lobster tails and continue to cook for 6 minutes until the flesh is opaque and the shells are red. Drain immediately and let cool completely.

5 Remove the lobster flesh from the shells and cut into bite-sized pieces. Arrange the radicchio leaves on individual plates and top with the lobster flesh. Place a spoonful of the lemon-dill mayonnaise on the side. Garnish with lemon wedges and dill sprigs and serve.

Pasta with Broccoli & Anchovy Sauce

Orecchiette, the cupped-shape pasta from southern Italy,
is excellent for this filling dish because it scoops up the robust, chunky sauce.

Serves 4

INGREDIENTS

1 lb. 2 oz. broccoli	2 large garlic cloves, crushed	2 oz. Parmesan cheese
14 oz. dried orecchiette	1¾ oz. can anchovy fillets in oil,	2 oz. pecorino cheese
5 tbsp. olive oil	drained and finely chopped	salt and pepper

1 Bring 2 pans of lightly salted water to a boil. Chop the broccoli florets and stems into small, bite-sized pieces. Add the broccoli to one pan and cook until very tender. Drain and set aside.

2 Put the pasta in the other pan of boiling water and cook for 10–12 minutes, or according to the instructions on the packet, until *al dente*.

3 Meanwhile, heat the olive oil in a large pan over medium heat. Add the garlic and fry for 3 minutes, stirring, without allowing it to brown. Add the chopped anchovies to the oil and cook for 3 minutes, stirring and mashing with a wooden spoon to break them up. Finely grate the Parmesan and pecorino cheeses.

4 Drain the pasta, add to the pan of anchovies, and stir. Add the broccoli and stir to mix.

5 Add the grated Parmesan and pecorino to the pasta and stir constantly over medium-high heat until the cheeses melt and the pasta and broccoli are coated.

6 Adjust the seasoning to taste—the anchovies and cheeses are salty, so you will only need to add pepper, if anything. Spoon into bowls or onto plates and serve at once.

VARIATIONS

Add dried chili flakes to taste with the garlic in Step 3, if you want. If you have difficulty in finding orecchiette, try using pasta bows instead.

Linguini with Pesto Sauce

The basil, olive oil, garlic, and pine nuts in this traditional pasta sauce are the essence of Italian Mediterranean cooking.

Serves 4; makes about 1 ¼ cups sauce

INGREDIENTS

14 oz. dried or fresh linguini
freshly grated Parmesan cheese, to
serve (optional)

PESTO SAUCE:
5½ oz. Parmesan cheese in a wedge
3 garlic cloves, or to taste
3 cups fresh basil leaves

5 tbsp. pine kernels (nuts)
⅔ cup fruity extra-virgin olive oil
salt and pepper

---

1 To make the pesto sauce, cut the rind off the Parmesan and finely grate the cheese. Set aside. Cut each garlic clove in half lengthwise and use the tip of the knife to lift out the green core, which can have a bitter flavor if the cloves are old. Coarsely chop the garlic.

2 Rinse the basil leaves and pat dry with paper towels. Put the basil in a food processor and add the pine nuts, grated cheese, chopped garlic and olive oil. Process for about 30 seconds, just until blended.

3 Add pepper and extra salt to taste, but cautiously— remember, the cheese is salty. Cover with a sheet of plastic wrap and chill for up to 5 days.

4 Bring a large pan of water to a boil. Add ½ teaspoon salt and the linguini and cook according to the packet instructions until *al dente*. Drain well, reserving a few tablespoons of the cooking water.

5 Return the linguini to the pan over low heat and stir in the sauce. Toss until well coated and the sauce is heated though. Stir in

a couple of tablespoons of the reserved cooking water if the sauce seems too thick. Serve at once with grated Parmesan for sprinkling over the top, if desired.

VARIATIONS

Pine nuts are a traditional ingredient, but blanched almonds can be used instead. To make a creamy dip to serve with sliced zucchini and bell pepper strips, stir 4 tablespoons of the pesto sauce into 4 tablespoons thick natural yogurt.

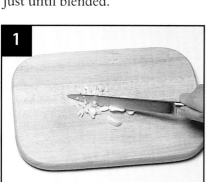

Spaghetti with Corsican Clam Sauce

Fresh mussels can also be used in this simple sauce.
Serve with a glass of chilled white wine.

Serves 4

INGREDIENTS

14 oz. dried or fresh spaghetti
salt and pepper

CORSICAN CLAM SAUCE:
2 lb. clams in their shells
4 tbsp. olive oil

3 large garlic cloves, crushed
pinch of dried chili flakes (optional)
2 lb. tomatoes, skinned and chopped,
   with juice reserved
2 oz. Flavored Olives (see page 172)
   of your choice, or plain green or

black olives, pitted and
   chopped
1 tbsp. chopped fresh oregano, or
   1/2 tsp. dried

1 Soak the clams in a bowl of lightly salted water for 30 minutes. Rinse them under cold, running water and lightly scrub to remove any sand from the shells.

2 Discard any broken clams or open clams that do not shut when firmly tapped with the back of a knife. This indicates that they are dead and could cause food poisoning if eaten. Soak the clams in a large bowl of water. Bring a large pan of lightly salted water to a boil.

3 Heat the oil in a skillet over medium heat. Add the garlic and chili flakes, if using, and fry for about 2 minutes.

4 Stir in the tomatoes, olives, and oregano. Lower the heat and simmer, stirring frequently, until the tomatoes soften and start to break up. Cover and simmer for 10 minutes.

5 Meanwhile, cook the spaghetti in the pan of boiling water according to the instructions on the packet until just *al dente*. Drain well, reserving about 1/2 cup of the cooking water. Keep the pasta warm.

6 Add the clams and reserved cooking liquid to the sauce and stir. Bring to a boil, stirring. Discard any clams that do not open, transfer to larger pan.

7 Add the pasta to the sauce and toss until well coated. Transfer the pasta to individual dishes. Serve at once.

Pasta with Tuna & Lemon

*Fusilli, corkscrew-shaped pasta, is the best shape to use for this recipe
because the creamy sauce is absorbed in the twists.*

Serves 4

INGREDIENTS

4 tbsp. butter, diced
1¼ cups heavy cream
4 tbsp. lemon juice
1 tbsp. grated lemon rind
½ tsp. anchovy extract

14 oz. dried fusilli
7 oz. can tuna in olive oil, drained
   and flaked
salt and pepper

TO GARNISH:
2 tbsp. finely chopped fresh parsley
zested lemon rind

1 Bring a large saucepan of lightly salted water to a boil. Melt the butter in a large skillet. Stir in the heavy cream and lemon juice and simmer, stirring, for about 2 minutes until slightly thickened.

2 Stir in the lemon rind and anchovy extract. Meanwhile, cook the pasta for 10–12 minutes or according to the instructions on the packet until just *al dente*. Drain well.

3 Add the sauce to the pasta and toss until well coated. Add the tuna and gently toss until well blended but not too broken up.

4 Season to taste with salt and pepper. Transfer to a serving platter and garnish with the parsley and lemon rind. Grind some pepper over the dish and serve at once.

COOK'S TIP

As an alternative, use the thin twist-shaped pasta, casareccia, instead.

VARIATIONS

For a vegetarian version, omit the tuna and anchovy extract. Add 5 oz. pitted olives instead. For extra "kick" add a pinch of dried chili flakes to the sauce instead of the anchovy extract.

Vegetables & Side Salads

The fresh produce from the Mediterranean is some of the most luscious and flavorful in the world. Slowly ripened under the hot Mediterranean sun, eggplants, zucchini, bell peppers, and tomatoes look so fantastic you can almost taste them with your eyes.

With such full flavors, you'll find the vegetable dishes are not complicated. For a Mediterranean touch, serve globe artichokes with a classic Hollandaise sauce flavored with blood-orange juice. Or, for another simple recipe, savor Fava Beans with Feta & Lemon—it's delicious served hot or cold. Charbroiled Vegetable Platter makes the most of fresh produce at its peak, while slow-cook stews, such as the classic Ratatouille, enhance the flavors of vegetables that are starting to pass their prime.

Salads feature prominently in Mediterranean meals, and there can't be many dishes more typically Mediterranean than Roasted Bell Pepper Salad or Mozzarella & Cherry Tomato Salad. Both have simple dressings and they make ideal accompaniments or first courses. And, at any time of the year, it's difficult to beat Panzanella, the Italian salad based on leftover bread and made into a colorful medley with refreshing tomatoes, cucumbers, and bell peppers.

Charbroiled Vegetable Platter

Charbroiling is a popular way of cooking vegetables throughout the Mediterranean because it intensifies the naturally strong flavor of the sun-ripened produce.

Serves 4–6

INGREDIENTS

4 lb. 8 oz. mixed fresh vegetables, such as eggplants, endive, zucchini, fennel, bell peppers, scallions

garlic-flavored olive oil
salt and pepper
fresh basil leaves, to garnish

1 Prepare the vegetables as necessary. Trim the ends of the eggplants and cut into ¼-inch slices. Cut each head of endive in half lengthwise.

2 Trim the ends from the zucchini and cut the zucchini into ¼-inch slices. Remove the fronds from the fennel and slice thickly across the grain.

3 Cut the bell peppers into quarters, then remove the cores and seeds. Trim the top green part of the scallions, and cut in half lengthwise if large.

4 As each vegetable is prepared, put it in a large bowl, drizzle with the garlic oil, and season lightly with salt and pepper. Using your hands, toss the vegetables together, so they are lightly coated with oil; the vegetables should not be dripping in oil.

5 Heat a large, ridged cast-iron skillet over high heat. Lightly brush with oil. Add a batch of vegetables—enough to fit in the pan in a single layer. Cook the vegetables on one side over medium-high heat until they are starting to turn limp.

6 Brush the half-cooked vegetables with a little more oil, then turn them. Continue cooking until they are tender—the exact cooking times will depend on the age and thickness of the vegetables. Transfer to a large platter and repeat with the remaining vegetables.

7 While still hot, sprinkle with salt and pepper. Garnish with basil leaves and serve.

Ratatouille

A slow-cooked Provençal vegetable stew, this goes particularly well with roast lamb, but is also excellent with any broiled meat or poultry.

Serves 4–6

INGREDIENTS

1 large eggplant, about 10½ oz.
5 tbsp. olive oil
2 large onions, thinly sliced
2 large garlic cloves, crushed
4 zucchini, sliced

2 x 14 oz. cans chopped tomatoes
1 tsp sugar
1 bouquet garni of 2 sprigs fresh
    thyme, 2 large sprigs parsley,
    1 sprig basil, and 1 bay leaf, tied in
    a 3-inch piece of celery

salt and pepper
fresh basil leaves, to garnish

1 Coarsely chop the eggplant, then place in a colander. Sprinkle with salt and allow to drain for 30 minutes. Rinse well and pat dry.

2 Heat the oil in a large heavy-based flameproof casserole over medium heat. Add the onions, lower the heat and fry, stirring frequently, for 10 minutes.

3 Add the garlic and continue to fry for 2 minutes until the onions are very tender, and lightly browned.

4 Add the eggplant, zucchini, tomatoes and their juice, the sugar, bouquet garni, and salt and pepper to taste. Bring to a boil, then lower the heat to very low, cover and simmer for 30 minutes.

5 Adjust the seasoning. Remove and discard the bouquet garni. Garnish the vegetable stew with basil leaves and serve.

COOK'S TIP

This is equally good served hot, at room temperature, or chilled. To make a vegetarian meal, serve it over cooked couscous (see page 80), or with Green Tabbouleh (see page 166).

Artichokes with Sauce Maltaise

Artichokes are often served with hollandaise sauce, the sharpness of the sauce complementing their distinctive flavor. Here the sauce is given a Mediterranean flavor with the addition of blood-orange juice.

Serves 4

INGREDIENTS

4 large globe artichokes
2 lemon slices

SAUCE MALTAISE:
1 blood orange
175 g/6 oz./³⁄₄ cup butter
3 tbsp. water

2–3 tbsp. lemon juice
3 egg yolks*
salt and pepper

*Use pasteurized egg products, available where eggs are sold, to minimize the risk of salmonella.

1 To prepare the globe artichokes, bring lightly salted water to a boil in a pan large enough to hold the 4 artichokes upright. Add the lemon slices. Break off the stems and trim the bases of the artichokes so they are flat and will sit upright on a plate.

2 Put the artichokes in the pan and place a heatproof plate on top. Lower the heat and simmer for 20–25 minutes, until you can easily pull a leaf out.

3 Meanwhile, make the sauce. Finely grate the rind from the orange and squeeze 2 tablespoons orange juice. Put the butter in a saucepan over medium heat and melt, skimming the surface.

4 Put the water, 2 tablespoons of the lemon juice, and salt and pepper in a bowl set over a pan of simmering water, making sure the base of the bowl does not touch the water. Whisk until heated.

5 Whisk in the egg yolks, until blended and warmed through. Add the hot butter in a steady stream, whisking constantly until a thick, smooth sauce forms.

6 Stir in the orange rind and juice. Adjust the seasoning, adding extra lemon juice if necessary—the flavor should be sharp. Remove from the heat.

7 Drain the artichokes. Place each on a plate with a ramekin of the Sauce Maltaise. Place an empty bowl on the table for the leaves after they have been eaten.

COOK'S TIP

Pull out the leaves, starting with the outer layer; work inward, until you get to the thin purple leaves that are inedible. Dip the bottom of each leaf into the creamy sauce and scrape off the fleshy part with your teeth. Cut off the central core of leaves and the hairy choke to reveal the delicious bottom, that can be cut with a knife and fork.

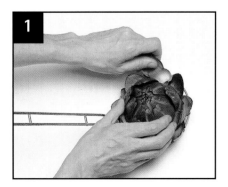

Baked Eggplant Gratin

Serve plenty of French bread with this dish because it produces the most delicious juices. It makes a flavorful vegetarian meal or an excellent accompaniment to broiled lamb.

Serves 4–6

INGREDIENTS

1 large eggplant, about
   1 lb. 12 oz.
salt
10½ oz. mozzarella cheese
3 oz. Parmesan cheese

olive oil
1 cup plus 2 tbsp. Slow-Cooked
   Tomato Sauce (see page 192), or
   good-quality canned tomato sauce
   for pasta

salt and pepper

1 Trim the ends from the eggplant and, using a sharp knife, cut into ¼-inch slices crosswise. Arrange the slices on a large plate, sprinkle with salt, and set aside for 30 minutes to drain.

2 Meanwhile, drain and grate the mozzarella cheese and finely grate the Parmesan cheese. Set aside.

3 Rinse the eggplant slices and pat dry with paper towels. Lightly brush a cookie sheet with olive oil and arrange the eggplant slices in a single layer. Brush the tops with olive oil.

4 Roast in a preheated oven at 400°F for 5 minutes. Using tongs, turn the slices, then brush with a little more oil and bake for a further 5 minutes, or until the eggplant is cooked through and tender. Do not turn off the oven.

5 Spread about 1 tablespoon olive oil over the bottom of a gratin dish or other ovenproof serving dish. Add a layer of eggplant slices, about a quarter of the tomato sauce, and top with a quarter of the mozzarella. Season to taste with salt and pepper.

6 Continue layering until all the ingredients are used, ending with a layer of sauce. Sprinkle the Parmesan over the top. Bake in the oven for 30 minutes until bubbling. Let it stand for 5 minutes before serving.

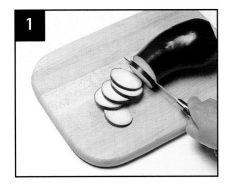

Imam Bayildi

The title of this traditional Turkish recipe means "the imam fainted," referring to a holy man who passed out with pleasure when presented with this dish, perhaps because of the wonderful aromas.

Serves 4

INGREDIENTS

2 eggplants, about 10½ oz. each
5 tbsp. olive oil
2 large onions, finely chopped
2 large garlic cloves, crushed
2 x 14 oz. cans chopped tomatoes
3 tbsp. raisins

3 tbsp. finely chopped fresh flat-leaf parsley
finely grated rind of ½ unwaxed lemon
2 tbsp. lemon juice
½ tsp ground cinnamon

½ tsp ground cumin
pinch of cayenne pepper
salt and pepper
fresh flat-leaf parsley sprigs, to garnish

1 Cut each eggplant in half lengthwise. Using a knife, scoop out the flesh from each half, leaving a ¼-inch shell all around. Set the shells aside.

2 Finely chop the eggplant flesh, place in a colander, sprinkle with salt, and allow to drain for 30 minutes. Rinse and pat dry.

3 Heat 3 tablespoons of the olive oil in a large skillet. Add the onions and fry, stirring frequently, over medium-high heat until softened. Add the garlic and continue frying for 2 minutes, stirring.

4 Add the tomatoes, eggplant flesh, raisins, parsley, lemon rind, lemon juice, cinnamon, cumin, and cayenne, then season with salt and pepper to taste. Simmer for 20 minutes, stirring occasionally, until the mixture has thickened.

5 Spoon the mixture into the eggplant shells, mounding it up slightly. Place the filled shells in an ovenproof dish and add the remaining olive oil.

6 Cover the dish with foil. Roast in a preheated oven at 350°F for 45–50 minutes until the eggplant shells are tender and the filling is hot. Serve hot, or let cool, then chill until required. Garnish with parsley.

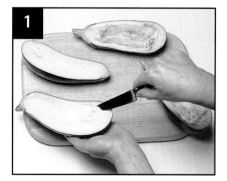

Sweet & Sour Zucchini

This versatile dish comes from English cookbook writer Jane Grigson's 1984 book, Dishes from the Mediterranean, *and has distinctly Middle Eastern flavorings.*

Serves 4–6

INGREDIENTS

1 lb. 2 oz. zucchini
3 tbsp. olive oil
1 large garlic clove, finely chopped
3 tbsp. red or white wine vinegar

3 tbsp. water
6–8 anchovy fillets, canned or salted
3 tbsp. pine nuts
1¼ oz. raisins

salt and pepper
fresh flat-leaf parsley sprigs, to garnish

1 Trim the ends from the zucchini, then use a sharp knife to cut them into long, thin strips. Heat the oil in a large skillet over medium heat. Add the garlic and fry, stirring, for about 2 minutes.

2 Add the zucchini and cook, stirring, until they just start to turn brown. Add the vinegar and water, cover, and simmer for 10 minutes, stirring.

3 Meanwhile, drain the anchovies if canned, or rinse if they are salted. Coarsely chop, then use the back of a wooden spoon to mash them to a paste.

4 Stir the anchovies, pine nuts, and raisins into the pan. Increase the heat and stir until the zucchini are bathed in a thin sauce and are tender. Adjust the seasoning, remembering that the anchovies are very salty.

5 Either serve at once, or allow to cool completely and serve at room temperature. To serve, garnish with fresh parsley sprigs.

VARIATION

Replace ordinary raisins with golden raisins. Add a little grated lemon or orange rind for zing.

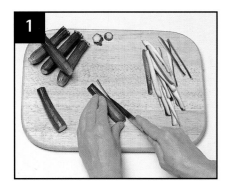

Deep-fried Zucchini

These crisp zucchini slices are so irresistible that you should always make more than you think you will need—they disappear very quickly!

Serves 4

INGREDIENTS

5 tbsp. cornstarch
1 tsp salt
pinch of cayenne pepper, or to taste

²/₃ cup water
2 lb. zucchini
vegetable oil, for frying

sea salt, to serve
fresh herb sprigs, such as basil, flat-leaf parsley, or sage, to garnish

1 Sift the corn flour, salt, and cayenne pepper into a large mixing bowl and make a well in the center. Pour in the water and beat until just blended to make a thin batter. The batter may have a few lumps but this does not matter. Set aside for 20 minutes.

2 Meanwhile, cut the zucchini into ¼-inch slices. Heat the oil in a deep skillet or deep-fat fryer to 375°F or until a cube of bread sizzles in 20 seconds.

3 Stir the batter. Working in batches, put some zucchini slices in the batter and stir around until coated. Using a slotted spoon, remove the slices from the batter, shaking off the excess.

4 Drop the coated zucchini slices into the hot fat and fry for about 45–60 seconds, or until just golden brown on each side. Immediately remove from the fat and drain well on crumpled paper towels. Sprinkle with sea salt and keep warm if not serving at once.

5 Repeat this process with the remaining zucchini slices. You can serve garnished with a variety of herbs.

COOK'S TIP

It is important to get the fat to the correct temperature— otherwise the fried zucchini will be soggy.

VARIATION

Fry red onion rings coated with the batter.

Braised Fennel

So important in Mediterranean cooking, fennel is often braised and served as a vegetable accompaniment to meat, poultry, or fish dishes. This dish is also very good with tomato salad.

Serves 4–6

INGREDIENTS

2 lemon slices
2 or 3 bulbs fennel, depending on
   size
1½ tbsp. olive oil

3 tbsp. butter
4 sprigs fresh thyme, or ½ tbsp.
   dried
¾ cup chicken or vegetable stock

1 cup freshly grated Parmesan
   cheese
pepper

1 Bring a large saucepan of water to a boil and add the lemon slices. Trim the fennel bulbs and slice each one lengthwise. Put them in a boiling water, bring back to a boil and simmer for about 8 minutes until almost tender. Drain well.

2 Put the oil and butter in a flameproof casserole and melt over medium heat. Swirl the melted mixture around so the bottom and sides of the casserole are well coated.

3 Add the fennel slices and stir until coated. Add the thyme and pepper to taste. Pour in the stock and sprinkle the cheese over the top.

4 Bake in a preheated oven at 400°F for 25–30 minutes until the fennel has absorbed the stock and is tender, and the cheese has melted and become golden brown. Serve at once.

COOK'S TIP

This is an ideal way to serve older fennel bulbs.

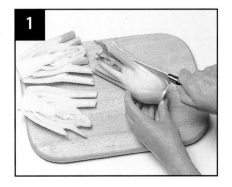

Mixed Vegetables à la Grecque

"A la Grecque" is the French term for cooked vegetables left to cool in the highly flavored cooking liquid and then served cold. This style of vegetable is very popular during hot Mediterranean summers.

Serves 4–6

INGREDIENTS

9 oz. small pickling onions
9 oz. mushrooms
9 oz. zucchini
2 cups water
5 tbsp. olive oil
2 tbsp. lemon juice

2 strips lemon rind
2 large garlic cloves, thinly sliced
½ Spanish onion, finely chopped
1 bay leaf
15 black peppercorns, lightly crushed
10 coriander seeds, lightly crushed

pinch of dried oregano
finely chopped fresh flat-leaf parsley
  or cilantro, to garnish
foccacia, to serve

1 Heat a kettle of water until the water boils. Put the small onions in a heatproof bowl and pour boiling water over them to cover. Let stand for 2 minutes, then drain. Peel and set aside.

2 Trim the mushroom stems; cut the mushrooms into halves or quarters if they are large, or leave whole. Trim the ends from the zucchini, cut off strips of the peel for a decorative finish, then cut into ¼-inch slices. Set both aside.

3 Put the water, olive oil, lemon juice and rind, garlic, Spanish onion, bay leaf, peppercorns, coriander seeds, and oregano in a saucepan over high heat and bring to a boil. Lower the heat and simmer for 15 minutes.

4 Add the small onions and continue to simmer for 5 minutes. Add the mushrooms and zucchini and simmer for a further 2 minutes. Using a slotted spoon, transfer all the vegetables to a heatproof dish.

5 Return the liquid to a boil and boil until reduced to about 6 tablespoons. Pour over the vegetables and set aside to cool completely.

6 Cover with plastic wrap and chill for at least 12 hours.

7 To serve, put the vegetables and cooking liquid in a serving dish and scatter the fresh herbs over them. Serve with chunks of foccacia.

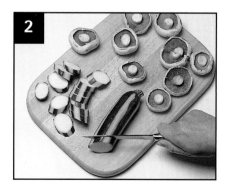

Glazed Baby Onions

These onions are bathed in a rich, intensely flavored glaze, making them a good accompaniment to any broiled or roasted meat.

Serves 4–6

INGREDIENTS

1 lb. 2 oz. pearl onions
2 tbsp. olive oil
2 large garlic cloves, crushed
1¼ cups vegetable or chicken
   stock

1 tbsp. fresh thyme leaves
1 tbsp. light brown sugar
2 tbsp. red wine vinegar
about ½ tbsp. best-quality balsamic
   vinegar

salt and pepper
fresh thyme sprigs, to garnish

1 Bring a kettle of water to a boil. Put the onions in a large heatproof bowl, pour over enough boiling water to cover, and let stand for 2 minutes. Drain well.

2 Using a small knife and your fingers, peel off the skins, which should slip off easily.

3 Heat the olive oil in a large skillet over medium-high heat.

4 Add the onions and cook, stirring, for about 8 minutes until they are golden on all sides.

5 Add the garlic and cook for 2 minutes, stirring. Add the stock, thyme leaves, sugar, and red wine vinegar, stirring until the sugar has dissolved.

6 Bring to a boil, then lower the heat and simmer for 10 minutes, or until the onions are tender when you pierce them with the tip of a knife and the cooking liquid is reduced to a syrupy glaze.

7 Stir in ½ tablespoon balsamic vinegar. Season to taste with salt and pepper and extra vinegar, if desired. Transfer to a serving dish and serve hot or cold, garnished with fresh thyme sprigs.

VARIATION

For extra texture, stir in 2 tablespoons toasted pine nuts just before serving. Do not add them earlier or they will become soft.

Spiced Lentils with Spinach

This dish is a good accompaniment to the broiled lamb and veal dishes, so popular throughout the Mediterranean. Serve with a tomato and onion salad for a vegetarian meal.

Serves 4–6

INGREDIENTS

2 tbsp. olive oil
1 large onion, finely chopped
1 large garlic clove, crushed
$1/2$ tbsp. ground cumin
$1/2$ tsp ground ginger
$1^3/4$ cups Puy lentils

about $2^1/2$ cups vegetable or chicken stock
$3^1/2$ oz. baby spinach leaves
2 tbsp. fresh mint leaves
1 tbsp. fresh cilantro leaves
1 tbsp. fresh flat-leaf parsley leaves

freshly squeezed lemon juice
salt and pepper
zested lemon rind, to garnish

1 Heat the olive oil in a large skillet over medium-high heat. Add the onion and cook for about 6 minutes. Stir in the garlic, cumin, and ginger and continue cooking, stirring occasionally, until the onion just starts to brown.

2 Stir in the lentils. Pour in enough stock to cover the lentils by 1 inch and bring to a boil. Lower the heat and simmer for 20 minutes, or according to the instructions

on the package, until the lentils are tender.

3 Meanwhile, rinse the spinach leaves in several changes of cold water and shake dry. Finely chop the mint, cilantro, and parsley leaves.

4 If there isn't any stock left in the pan, add a little extra. Add the spinach and stir through until it just wilts. Stir in the mint, cilantro, and parsley. Adjust the seasoning, adding lemon juice and

salt and pepper. Transfer to a serving bowl and serve, garnished with lemon rind.

COOK'S TIP

This recipe uses green lentils from Puy in France because they are good at keeping their shape even after long cooking. You can, however, also use orange or brown lentils, but it is necessary to watch them while they cook or they will quickly turn to a mush.

Borlotti Beans in Tomato Sauce

Fresh sage, an herb used frequently in Mediterranean cooking, adds a subtle flavor to these pink-and-white speckled beans, which are an Italian favorite.

Serves 4–6

INGREDIENTS

1 lb. 5 oz. fresh borlotti beans, in shells
4 large leaves fresh sage, torn
1 tbsp. olive oil

1 large onion, finely sliced
1¼ cups Slow-cooked Tomato Sauce (see page 192), or good-quality canned tomato sauce for pasta

salt and pepper
extra shredded sage leaves, to garnish

1 Shell the borlotti beans. Bring a saucepan of water to a boil, add the beans and torn sage leaves, and simmer for about 12 minutes, or until tender. Drain and set aside.

2 Heat the oil in a large skillet over medium heat. Add the onion and cook, stirring occasionally, for about 5 minutes until soft but not brown. Stir the tomato sauce into the pan with the cooked borlotti beans and the torn sage leaves.

3 Increase the heat and bring to a boil, stirring. Lower the heat, partially cover, and simmer for about 10 minutes, or until the the sauce has slightly reduced.

4 Adjust the seasoning, transfer to a serving bowl and serve hot, garnished with fresh sage leaves.

VARIATION

If fresh borlotti beans are unavailable, use 2 x 10 oz. cans instead. Drain and rinse, then add with the sage and tomato sauce in Step 2.

Fava Beans with Feta & Lemon

This simple dish captures the heady flavors of the Greek islands, and makes a good hot vegetable accompaniment to serve with barbecued lamb, or as a salad or cold first course.

Serves 4–6

INGREDIENTS

1 lb. 2 oz. shelled fava beans
4 tbsp. extra-virgin olive oil

1 tbsp. lemon juice
1 tbsp. finely chopped fresh dill, plus a little extra for garnishing

2 oz. feta cheese, drained and diced
salt and pepper
lemon wedges, to serve

1 Bring a saucepan of water to a boil. Add the fava beans and cook for about 2 minutes until tender. Drain well.

2 When the beans are cool enough to handle, remove and discard the outer skins, to reveal the bright green beans underneath (see Cook's Tip). Put the peeled beans in a serving bowl.

3 Stir together the olive oil and lemon juice, then season to taste with salt and pepper. Pour over the warm beans, add the dill and stir together. Adjust the seasoning, if necessary.

4 If serving hot, toss with the feta cheese and sprinkle with extra dill. Alternatively, let cool, then chill until required. Remove from the refrigerator 10 minutes before serving, season, then sprinkle with the feta and extra dill. Serve with lemon wedges.

COOK'S TIP

If you are lucky enough to have very young fava beans at the start of the season, it isn't necessary to remove the outer skin.

COOK'S TIP

It's worth using a good-quality olive oil, as it will make all the difference to the flavor of the finished dish.

Mozzarella & Cherry Tomato Salad

*Take advantage of the delicious varieties of cherry tomatoes that are available
to make a refreshing Italian-style salad with lots of eye appeal!*

Serves 4–6

INGREDIENTS

1 lb. cherry tomatoes	7 oz. buffalo mozzarella (see Cook's	salt and pepper
4 scallions	Tip), cut into cubes	
1/2 cup extra-virgin olive oil	1/2 oz. fresh flat-leaf parsley	
2 tbsp. best-quality balsamic vinegar	1 oz. fresh basil leaves	

1 Using a sharp knife, cut the tomatoes in half and put in a large bowl. Trim the scallions and finely chop the green and white parts, then add to the bowl.

2 Pour in the olive oil and balsamic vinegar and use your hands to toss together. Season with salt and pepper, add the mozzarella, and toss again. Cover and chill for 4 hours.

3 Remove from the refrigerator 10 minutes before serving. Finely chop the parsley and add to the salad. Tear the basil leaves

over the salad and toss all the ingredients together again. Adjust the seasoning and serve.

COOK'S TIP

For the best flavor, buy buffalo mozzarella—mozzarella di bufala—rather than the factory-made cow's milk version. This salad would also look good made with bocconcini, which are small balls of mozzarella. Look for these in Italian delicatessens.

VARIATIONS

Replace the cherry tomatoes with Oven-dried Tomatoes (see page 174), or drained sun-dried tomatoes soaked in oil.

To make this salad more substantial, stir in 14 oz. cooked and cooled pasta shapes. When the pasta is al dente, drain well and toss with 1 tablespoon olive oil and cool completely before adding to the tomatoes and mozzarella in Step 1.

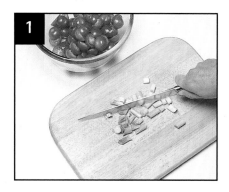

Roasted Bell Pepper Salad

Large, intensely flavored sweet bell peppers are sold in abundance throughout the Mediterranean during the summer months. This is a classic way of preparing them.

Serves 4–6

INGREDIENTS

4–6 large red, yellow, and/or orange
  bell peppers
2 scallions, trimmed

LEMON-PARSLEY VINAIGRETTE:
6 tbsp. extra-virgin olive oil
1¹/₂ tbsp. freshly squeezed lemon juice

2 tbsp. finely chopped fresh flat-leaf
  parsley
salt and pepper

1 To make the dressing, put the oil, lemon juice, and parsley in a screw-top jar and shake until well blended. Add salt and pepper to taste. Set aside.

2 Slice the tops off the (bell) peppers, then cut each into quarters or thirds, depending on the size. Remove the cores and seeds—the flatter the pieces are, the easier they are to cook.

3 Finely slice the scallions on the diagonal.

4 Place the bell pepper pieces on a broiler rack under a preheated hot broiler and broil for about 10 minutes, or until the skins are charred and the flesh is softened.

5 Using tongs, remove each piece as it is ready. Immediately place in a bowl and cover with plastic wrap. Set aside for 20 minutes to allow the steam to loosen the skins.

6 When cool, carefully use a small, sharp knife or your fingers, to remove all of the skins from the bell peppers, then slice the bell pepper flesh into long, thin strips.

7 Arrange the bell pepper strips on a serving platter. Shake the dressing again, then pour over the salad. Scatter the scallions over the top. Serve with crusty bread, or cover and chill until required.

VARIATIONS

For a party, marinate small, cooked shrimp in the dressing and scatter them over the salad. Other Mediterranean ingredients you can add to the salad include capers, anchovies, pitted and sliced green or black olives, and finely grated lemon rind.

Stuffed Tomato Salad

*Make this at the height of summer when it is too hot to cook and juicy,
sun-ripened, extra-large tomatoes are at their peak, bursting with flavor.*

Makes 4

INGREDIENTS

about 1½ oz. cucumber, finely
   diced
3 large eggs
4 extra-large tomatoes, about
   10½ oz. each

5 scallions, trimmed and diced
12 oz. can tuna in olive oil,
   drained
1–2 tbsp. mayonnaise
squeeze of lemon juice

small handful of basil leaves, plus
   extra for garnishing
salt and pepper

1 Put the cucumber in a plastic strainer, sprinkle with salt, and drain for 30 minutes.

2 Meanwhile, bring a pan of water to a boil, add the eggs, and cook for 12 minutes. Drain and place under running cold water to stop the cooking process.

3 Shell the eggs and chop the yolks and whites separately. Rinse the cucumber and pat dry with paper towels.

4 Working with one tomato at a time, slice off the top and use a small spoon to scoop out the insides; reserve the insides. Drain the tomatoes upside-down on paper towels. Chop the reserved scooped-out insides and drain.

5 Put the chopped tomato in a bowl and add the chopped cucumber, diced scallions, all the egg yolks, and most of the egg white, reserving a little to sprinkle over the tops. Flake in the tuna.

6 Add 1 tablespoon of the mayonnaise, the lemon juice, and salt and pepper to taste. Stir together and add a little more mayonnaise if the mixture is too thick. Tear in the basil leaves and stir together. Adjust the seasoning, if necessary.

7 Spoon the filling into the hollowed-out tomatoes. Sprinkle the tops with the reserved egg white. Cover with plastic wrap and chill until required, but not for more than 3 hours or the filling will become soggy. Garnish with basil leaves before serving.

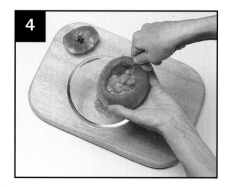

Panzanella

This traditional, refreshing Italian salad of day-old bread is ideal to serve for lunch or as a simple supper on a hot day. It is packed with Mediterranean flavors and very easy to put together.

Serves 4–6

INGREDIENTS

9 oz. stale Herb Foccacia (see page 206) or ciabatta bread or French bread

4 large, vine-ripened tomatoes

extra-virgin olive oil

4 red, yellow, and/or orange bell peppers

3½ oz. cucumber

1 large red onion, finely chopped

8 canned anchovy fillets, drained and chopped

2 tbsp. capers in brine, rinsed and patted dry

about 4 tbsp. red wine vinegar

about 2 tbsp. best-quality balsamic vinegar

salt and pepper

fresh basil leaves, to garnish

1 Cut the bread into 1-inch cubes and place in a large bowl. Working over a plate to catch any juices, quarter the tomatoes; reserve the juices. Using a teaspoon, scoop out the cores and seeds, then finely chop the flesh. Add to the bread cubes.

2 Drizzle 5 tablespoons of olive oil over the mixture and toss with your hands until well coated. Pour in the reserved tomato juice and toss again. Set aside for about 30 minutes.

3 Meanwhile, cut the bell peppers in half and remove the cores and seeds. Place on a broiler rack under a preheated hot broiler and broil for 10 minutes, or until the skins are charred and the flesh softened. Place in a plastic bag, seal, and set aside for 20 minutes to allow the steam to loosen the skins. Remove the skins, then finely chop.

4 Cut the cucumber in half lengthwise, then cut each half into 3 strips lengthwise. Using a

teaspoon, scoop out and discard the seeds. Dice the cucumber.

5 Add the onion, peppers, cucumber, anchovy fillets, and capers to the bread and toss together. Sprinkle with the red wine and balsamic vinegars and season to taste with salt and pepper. Drizzle with extra olive oil or vinegar if necessary, but be cautious that it does not become too greasy or soggy. Sprinkle the fresh basil leaves over the salad and serve at once.

Green Tabbouleh

Tomatoes are sometimes included in this refreshing bulgar wheat salad from Turkey, but this version relies on green herbs and vegetables for its flavor.

Serves 4

INGREDIENTS

1¼ cups bulgar wheat
7 oz. cucumber
6 scallions

½ oz. fresh flat-leaf parsley
1 unwaxed lemon

about 2 tbsp. garlic-flavored olive oil
salt and pepper

1 Bring a kettle of water to a boil. Place the bulgar wheat in a heatproof bowl, pour 2 ½ cups boiling water over, and cover with an upturned plate. Set aside for at least 20 minutes until the wheat absorbs the water and becomes tender.

2 While the wheat is soaking, cut the cucumber in half lengthwise and then cut each half into 3 strips lengthwise. Using a teaspoon, scoop out and discard the seeds. Chop the cucumber strips into bite-sized pieces. Put the cucumber pieces in a serving bowl.

3 Trim the top of the green parts of each of the scallions, then cut each in half lengthwise. Finely chop and add to the cucumber.

4 Place the parsley on a chopping board and sprinkle with salt. Using a cook's knife, very finely chop both the leaves and stems. Add to the bowl with the cucumber and onions. Finely grate the lemon rind into the bowl.

5 When the bulgar wheat is cool enough to handle, either squeeze out any excess water with your hands or press out the water through a strainer, then add to the bowl with the other ingredients.

6 Cut the lemon in half and squeeze the juice of one half over the salad. Add 2 tablespoons of the garlic-flavored oil and stir all the ingredients together. Adjust the seasoning with salt and pepper to taste and extra lemon juice or oil if needed. Cover and chill until required.

COOK'S TIP

Serve as part of a meze with dips such as Hummus (see page 8).

Radicchio & Bacon Salad

Cooked radicchio isn't that familiar outside Italy, but its slightly crunchy texture makes it an ideal ingredient to include in warm salads. This is a rich dish, so a little goes a long way.

Serves 4–6

INGREDIENTS

1 lb. 5 oz. radicchio, 3 or 4 heads, depending on size
about 3 tbsp. olive oil

1 large garlic clove, crushed
10½ oz. bacon
about 1 tbsp. best-quality balsamic vinegar

salt and pepper
fresh basil leaves, to garnish

1 Remove enough of the outer leaves from the radicchio heads to line 4–6 individual plates. Cut the remaining radicchio across the grain into ¼ inch slices.

2 Heat 3 tablespoons of oil in a large skillet over medium-high heat. Add the garlic clove and fry, stirring, for 2 minutes. Remove from the pan with a slotted spoon.

3 Add the bacon and fry for about 5 minutes, or until cooked through and brown on the outside. Do not overcook.

4 Add the shredded radicchio to the pan and toss for about 30 seconds, just until it is heated through and starting to become limp but not long enough to become soggy (see Cook's Tip).

5 Add 1 tablespoon of the balsamic vinegar and toss again. Drizzle with extra oil or vinegar, if desired. Add salt and pepper to taste. Spoon the hot salad on to the radicchio-lined plates and garnish with fresh basil leaves. Serve at once.

COOK'S TIP

It is important not to overcook the radicchio in Step 4 or it will become gray. Just warm it through.

Accompaniments

You'll find a collection of diverse recipes in this chapter. These are the recipes that help you add a Mediterranean flavor to any meal you serve. Use the Mediterranean Fish Stock, for example, when you want to make a soup with subtle, authentic flavoring, or make Flavored Olives, preserved in olive oil, to have on hand when friends stop by for a drink.

Wherever you live, the chances are that there will be a glut of tomatoes at some time. Try the Mediterranean trick of slow-roasting the tomatoes, then storing them in olive oil so you can add their fresh flavor to pasta sauces and casseroles throughout the year. Or, make large batches of Slow-cooked Tomato Sauce and stock the freezer.

The breads in this chapter are flavored with some of the region's most distinctive flavorings—Herb Foccacia makes a good accompaniment to any meal; Olive Rolls have so much flavor they can be munched on their own or made into delicious sandwiches; and Sesame Breadsticks, soft on the inside with a crisp exterior, disappear in a flash when served with one of the creamy dips.

Greeks, Cypriots, and Turks, in particular, enjoy thick, creamy yogurt with just about every meal of the day. In some parts of the world this is readily available in supermarkets, but if you can't get it, follow the recipe in this chapter for Greek Strained Yogurt.

Flavored Olives

In the weekly street markets that characterize Mediterranean life, you are sure to find stalls selling flavored olives. Ingredients vary with the regions—here are three ideas.

Each fills a 2¼ cup preserving jar

INGREDIENTS

fresh herb sprigs, such as cilantro, flat-leaf parsley, or thyme, to serve

PROVENCAL-STYLE OLIVES:
3 dried red chilies
1 tsp. black peppercorns
300 g/10½ oz. black Niçoise olives in brine
2 lemon slices
1 tsp. black mustard seeds
1 tbsp. garlic-flavored olive oil
fruity extra-virgin olive oil

CATALAN-STYLE OLIVES:
½ grilled red or orange bell pepper (see page 164)
5½ oz. black olives in brine
5½ oz. green pimento-stuffed olives in brine
1 tbsp. capers in brine, rinsed
pinch of dried chili flakes, or to taste
4 tbsp. coarsely chopped fresh cilantro leaves
1 bay leaf
fruity extra-virgin olive oil

CRACKED GREEK-STYLE OLIVES:
½ large lemon
10½ oz. kalamata olives in brine
4 sprigs fresh thyme
1 shallot, very finely chopped
1 tbsp. fennel seeds, lightly crushed
1 tsp. dried dill
fruity extra-virgin olive oil

1 To make the Provençal-style olives, place the dried red chilies and black peppercorns in a mortar and lightly crush. Drain and rinse the olives, then pat dry with paper towels. Put all the ingredients in a 2¼-cup preserving jar, pouring over enough olive oil to cover.

2 Seal the jar and leave for at least 10 days before serving, shaking the jar daily.

3 To make the Catalan-style olives, finely chop the bell pepper. Drain and rinse both olives, then pat dry with paper towels. Put all the ingredients into a

2¼-cup preserving jar, pouring over enough olive oil to cover. Seal and marinate as in Step 2.

4 To make the cracked Greek-style olives, cut the lemon into 4 slices, then cut each slice into wedges. Drain and rinse the olives, then pat dry with paper towels.

5 Slice each olive lengthwise on one side down to the pit. Put all the ingredients in a 2¼-cup preserving jar, pouring over olive oil to cover. Seal and marinate as in Step 2.

6 To serve, spoon into a bowl and garnish with fresh herbs.

Oven-dried Tomatoes

When you can't take advantage of the intense Mediterranean sun, use this easy technique to preserve tomatoes' rich flavor. Only use ripe, full-flavored tomatoes for this.

Makes enough to fill a generous 1-cup preserving jar

INGREDIENTS

2 lb. 4 oz. large, juicy full-flavored tomatoes	sea salt extra-virgin olive oil

1 Using a sharp knife, cut each of the tomatoes into quarters lengthwise.

2 Using a teaspoon, scoop out the seeds and discard. If the tomatoes are large, cut each quarter in half lengthwise again.

3 Sprinkle sea salt in a roasting pan and arrange the tomato slices, skin-side down, on top. Roast in a preheated oven at 250°F for 2½ hours, or until the edges are just starting to look charred and the flesh is dry but still pliable. The exact roasting time and yield will depend on the size and juiciness of the tomatoes.

Check the tomatoes at 30-minute intervals after 1½ hours.

4 Remove the dried tomatoes from the pan and cool completely. Put into a 1-cup preserving jar and pour over enough olive oil to cover. Seal tightly and store in the refrigerator for up to 2 weeks.

COOK'S TIP

Serve these oven-dried tomatoes with slices of buffalo mozzarella: drizzle with olive oil and sprinkle with coarsely ground black pepper and finely torn basil leaves.
Add a few slices of oven-roasted tomatoes to the ingredients in Slow-cooked Tomato Sauce (see page 192) while the ingredients are simmering for extra depth of flavor. Or add thin slices of these tomatoes to Salade Niçoise (see page 118), or Roasted Bell Pepper Salad (see page 160).

Preserved Citrus

A piece of citrus fruit preserved by an age-old method is often used in Mediterranean stews to give an intriguing hint of flavor—preserved lemons are an essential ingredient in many Moroccan tagines, and dried orange rind is included in the best Provençal daubes.

Preserved Lemons: makes enough to fill a 8-cup preserving jar
Dried Orange Rind: makes 1 long strip

INGREDIENTS

PRESERVED LEMONS:
4 large, thin-skinned unwaxed lemons

about 4 lb. 8 oz. table salt
4 bay leaves

DRIED ORANGE RIND:
1 large, unwaxed sweet orange

1 To make the preserved lemons, rinse the lemons with warm water, then pat dry with paper towels. Stand a lemon on its stem end, then cut it into quarters without cutting all the way through. Repeat with the 3 lemons.

2 Spread a ¼-inch layer of salt on the bottom of a 8-cup preserving jar with a non-metallic lid. Add one of the lemons, cut-side up, pressing to open out the quarters. Add a bay leaf and enough salt to completely cover. Repeat to make 3 more layers.

3 Using a wooden spoon, press down on the lemons to release their juice. Cover with a layer of salt. Seal the jar and set aside for at least a month, turning the jar upside-down every day.

4 Pull out a lemon quarter when required and rinse well. To use, follow the specific recipe instructions—some recipes use the flesh as well as the rind, while others use only the rind.

5 To make the dried orange rind, use a small, serrated knife to cut the rind off a large

orange in a single spiral, starting from the top and working your way to the bottom.

6 Thread a needle with thin thread and stitch it through the orange rind to make a loop to hang the rind from. Hang the rind from a nail in your kitchen until it is dry. Store in an airtight jar and use as required.

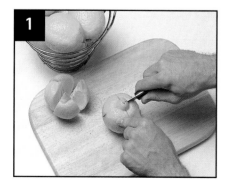

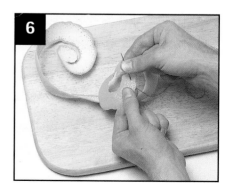

Candied Citrus Peel

*The intense Mediterranean sun produces some of the most flavorful citrus fruit in the world,
and this is one traditional way to preserve the peel.*

Makes 60–80 pieces

INGREDIENTS

1 large unwaxed, thick-skinned orange
1 large unwaxed, thick-skinned lemon
1 large unwaxed, thick-skinned lime

3 cups superfine sugar
1¼ cups water

4½ oz. best-quality dark chocolate,
   chopped (optional)

1 Cut the orange into quarters lengthwise and squeeze the juice into a cup to drink, or use in another recipe. Cut each quarter in half lengthwise to make 8 pieces.

2 Cut the fruit and pith away from the rind. If any of the pith remains on the rind, lay the knife almost flat on the white-side of the rind and gently "saw" backward and forward to slice it off because it will taste bitter.

3 Repeat with the lemon and lime, but cut the lime into quarters only. Cut each piece into 3 or 4 thin strips to make 60–80

strips in total. Place the strips in a pan of water and boil for 30 seconds. Drain.

4 Dissolve the sugar in the water in a pan over medium heat, stirring. Increase the heat and bring to a boil, without stirring. When the syrup becomes clear, turn the heat to its lowest setting.

5 Add the citrus strips, using a wooden spoon to push them in without stirring. Simmer in the syrup for 30 minutes without stirring. Turn off the heat and set aside for at least 6 hours until completely cool.

6 Line a cookie sheet with kitchen foil. Skim off the thin crust on top of the syrup without stirring. Remove the rind strips, one by one, from the syrup, shaking off any excess. Place the strips on the foil to cool.

7 If you want to dip candied peel in chocolate, melt the chocolate. Working with one piece of candied peel at a time, dip the peel halfway into the chocolate. Return to the foil and let dry. Store in an airtight container.

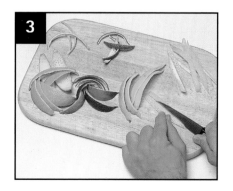

Mediterranean Fish Stock

Use this to give body and depth of flavor to Mediterranean soups. Flat fish bones and heads are traditionally used to make fish stocks because of the gelatin in the bones. Sole and flounder are ideal, but you can use whatever is available, except oily fish bones and trimmings.

Makes about 8 cups

INGREDIENTS

2 lb. 4 oz. fish bones and
    trimmings
at least 13 cups water
pinch of salt

4 large tomatoes
2 large bulbs of fennel
2 large garlic cloves
1 leek

1 bouquet garni of 2 sprigs fresh flat-
    leaf parsley and 1 sprig fresh thyme,
    tied in a 3-inch piece celery
1/2 cup dry white wine

1 Rinse the fish bones and trimmings under running cold water, wiping off any blood. Place them in a large flameproof casserole or stockpot and pour the water over them. Add a pinch of salt and heat until almost boiling, with bubbles just breaking the surface, but do not let the liquid boil.

2 Using a large spoon, skim the surface. Lower the heat to the lowest setting and simmer the stock, uncovered, for 30 minutes, skimming the surface as necessary.

3 Meanwhile, chop the tomatoes, fennel, and garlic. Slice the leek, then chop and rinse well in a bowl of cold water. Drain well.

4 Strain the fish stock into a large bowl and discard the solids.

5 Return the stock to the washed-out casserole or stockpot and add the vegetables, bouquet garni, and wine. Slowly bring to a boil, skimming the surface with a spoon as necessary.

6 Lower the heat, partially cover, and simmer for a further 30 minutes, or until reduced to about 8 cups. Strain the stock into a large bowl and cool.

COOK'S TIP

*This will keep
in the refrigerator,
covered, for 2 days.*

Greek Strained Yogurt

Smooth and creamy, this Greek-style yogurt makes a refreshing start to hot days, spread on pita bread for breakfast, or as a dip for an afternoon snack with drinks.

Makes about 2¼ cups

INGREDIENTS

2 lb. 4 oz. natural yogurt
½ tsp. salt, or to taste

OPTIONAL TOPPINGS:
fruity extra-virgin olive oil
orange-blossom or lavender-flavored
  honey
coriander seeds, crushed

paprika
very finely chopped fresh mint or
  cilantro
finely grated lemon rind

1 Place a 50 x 30-inch piece of cheesecloth in a saucepan, cover with water, and bring to a boil. Remove the pan from the heat and, using a wooden spoon, lift out the cheesecloth. Wearing gloves, wring the cloth dry.

2 Fold the cloth into a double layer and use it to line a colander or strainer set over a large bowl. Put the yogurt in a bowl and stir in the salt. Spoon the yogurt into the center of the cloth.

3 Tie the cloth so it is suspended above the bowl. If your sink is deep enough, gather up the corners of the cloth and tie it to the faucet. If not, lay a broom handle across 2 chairs and put the bowl between the chairs. Tie the cloth to the broom handle. Remove the colander or strainer and let the yogurt drain into the bowl for at least 12 hours.

4 Transfer the thickened drained yogurt to a plastic strainer sitting in a bowl. Cover

lightly with plastic wrap and keep in the refrigerator for another 24 hours until soft and creamy. This will keep refrigerated for up to 5 days.

5 To serve, taste and add extra salt if needed. Spoon the yogurt into a bowl and sprinkle with the topping of your choice, or a combination of toppings.

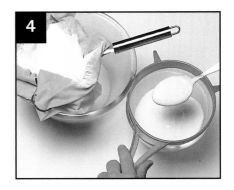

Aioli

This garlic mayonnaise features in many traditional Provençal recipes, but also makes a delicious dip, surrounded by a selection of raw and lightly cooked vegetables.

Makes about 1½ cups

INGREDIENTS

4 large garlic cloves, or to taste
pinch of sea salt
2 large egg yolks*
1¼ cups extra-virgin olive oil
1–2 tbsp. lemon juice, to taste

1 tbsp. fresh white breadcrumbs
freshly ground black pepper

TO SERVE (OPTIONAL):
a selection of raw vegetables, such as
  sliced red bell peppers, zucchini

slices, whole scallions, and tomato
wedges
a selection of blanched and cooled
vegetables, such as baby artichoke
hearts, cauliflower or broccoli
florets, or green beans

*Use pasteurized egg products, available where eggs are sold, to minimize the risk of salmonella.

1 Finely chop the garlic on a chopping board. Add the salt to the garlic and use the tip and broad side of a knife to work the garlic and salt into a smooth paste.

2 Transfer the garlic paste to a food processor. Add the egg yolks and process until well blended, scraping down the side of the bowl with a rubber spatula, if necessary.

3 With the motor running, slowly pour in the olive oil in a steady steam through the feed tube, processing until a thick mayonnaise forms.

4 Add 1 tablespoon of the lemon juice and the fresh breadcrumbs and quickly process again. Taste and add more lemon juice if necessary. Season to taste with salt and pepper.

5 Place the aioli in a bowl, cover, and chill until ready to serve. This will keep for up to 7 days in the refrigerator. To serve as a dip, place the bowl of aioli on a large platter and surround with a selection of crudités.

COOK'S TIP

The amount of garlic in a traditional Provençal aioli is a matter of personal taste. Local cooks use 2 cloves per person as a rule of thumb, but this version is slightly milder, although still bursting with flavor.

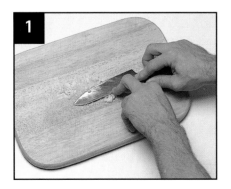

Rouille

No Provençal seafood soup is complete without this fiery red, thick sauce spread on croutons for floating on the surface. Modern recipes tend to be based on a chili-flavored mayonnaise, but this traditional, rustic version does not contain eggs.

Makes about ¾ cup

INGREDIENTS

2 oz. day-old country-style white bread

2 large garlic cloves

2 small red chilies

pinch of salt

3 tbsp. extra-virgin olive oil

1 tbsp. tomato paste

cayenne pepper (optional)

pepper

1 Cut the crusts off the bread. Put the bread in a bowl, pour water over it to cover, and soak for 30 seconds, or until soft. Squeeze the bread dry, reserving 2 tablespoons of the soaking liquid.

2 Coarsely chop the garlic and chilies. Put them in a mortar with a pinch of salt and pound until they form a paste.

3 Add the paste to the squeezed bread, then continue working in the mortar until the ingredients blend together. Transfer to a bowl and slowly add the olive oil, beating constantly. If the mixture begins to separate, add a little of the reserved soaking liquid and continue beating.

4 Add the tomato paste and cayenne pepper to taste. Adjust seasoning.

COOK'S TIP

If the sauce appears to be separating after it has stood for a while, stir in 1 tablespoon hot water. If it appears too thin to spread on croutons, beat in a little extra soaked bread.

VARIATION

For a smoother version, use a small food processor. Put the squeezed bread and chopped garlic and chilies in the food processor and blend. Add the olive oil and tomato paste and blend again until smooth. Adjust the seasoning.

Skordalia

This thick Greek almond and garlic sauce is the traditional accompaniment to broiled fish and meat.
It also makes an ideal dip to serve with crudités and Sesame Breadsticks (see page 200).

Makes about 1½ cups

INGREDIENTS

2 oz. day-old bread in one piece
1¼ cups unblanched almonds

4–6 large garlic cloves, coarsely
chopped
⅔ cup extra-virgin olive oil
2 tbsp. white wine vinegar

salt and pepper
sprigs fresh cilantro or flat-leaf
parsley, to garnish

1 Cut the crusts off the bread and tear the bread into small pieces. Put in a bowl, pour enough water over to cover, and soak for 10–15 minutes. Squeeze the bread dry; set aside.

2 To blanch the almonds, bring a kettle of water to a boil. Put the almonds in a heatproof bowl and pour enough boiling water over just to cover. Let stand for 30 seconds, then drain. The skins should slide off easily.

3 Transfer the almonds and garlic to a food processor and process until finely chopped. Add the squeezed bread and process again until well blended.

4 With the motor running, slowly add the olive oil through the feed tube in a steady stream until a thick paste forms. Add the vinegar and process again. Season with salt and pepper to taste.

5 Transfer to a bowl, cover and chill until required. This will keep in the refrigerator for up to 4 days. To serve, garnish with the fresh herb sprigs.

VARIATIONS

Many versions of this rustic sauce exist. For variety, replace the bread with 4 tablespoons well-drained canned cannellini or fava beans. You can replace the white wine vinegar with freshly squeezed lemon juice.

Fresh Tomato Sauce

This is the sauce to make when you have a glut of flavor-packed tomatoes. Fresh basil has a natural affinity with tomatoes, but you can also use other herbs, such as cilantro, mint, oregano, or thyme.

Makes enough to fill two 2¼ cup jars

INGREDIENTS

2 lb. 4 oz. juicy plum tomatoes
4–6 tbsp. extra-virgin olive oil
2 tsp. sugar

3 tbsp. finely torn fresh basil or
  flat-leaf parsley
salt and pepper

pasta shapes, such as fusilli or shells,
  to serve (optional)

1 Bring a kettle of water to a boil. Cut a small X in the top of each tomato and place in 1 or 2 heatproof bowls. Pour the water over and leave for 1 minute, then drain. Work in batches if necessary.

2 Peel off the skins and discard, working over a strainer placed over a bowl to catch and strain the tomato juices. Quarter all the tomatoes and remove the seeds. Coarsely chop the tomato flesh into bite-sized cubes.

3 Put the tomatoes and their juice in a bowl. Add 4 tablespoons of the olive oil, with the sugar and reserved tomato juice. Season with salt and pepper to taste. Gently stir together, adding a little more olive oil if it is too thick. Let the sauce stand for at least 30 minutes before using.

4 When ready to serve, stir in the fresh herbs. Serve with pasta shapes.

COOK'S TIP

When tomatoes are not at their peak, Slow-cooked Tomato Sauce (see page 192) is a better option.

COOK'S TIP

If you make the sauce in advance, cover and chill for up to 3 days. Twenty minutes before serving, remove from the refrigerator to let the sauce come to room temperature. Stir in the herbs just before serving.

Slow-cooked Tomato Sauce

Good-quality canned tomatoes will do for this all-purpose sauce. Its smooth texture makes it suitable for topping pizzas, as well as serving with spaghetti and other noodle dishes.

Makes about 2½ cups

INGREDIENTS

2 sprigs fresh parsley	2 tbsp. olive oil	½ tsp. sugar
2 sprigs fresh thyme	1 large garlic clove, crushed	salt and pepper
1 bay leaf	3½ oz. shallots, chopped	
3-inch piece of celery	1¼ cups full-bodied red wine	
1 kg/2 lb. 4 oz. plum tomatoes	2 strips freshly pared lemon rind	

1 To make the bouquet garni, use a piece of kitchen string to tie the sprigs of parsley and thyme and the bay leaf in the piece of celery. Set aside.

2 Coarsely chop the tomatoes—it isn't necessary to remove the skins or seeds because this sauce will be processed in a food mill, which will result in a smooth texture.

3 Heat the olive oil in a deep skillet with a lid or a saucepan. Add the garlic and shallots and cook for about 3 minutes, stirring with a wooden spoon, until softened.

4 Add the tomatoes, wine, bouquet garni, lemon rind, sugar, and salt and pepper to taste. Bring to a boil, stirring. Lower the heat, partially cover, and simmer very gently for 1 hour, or until most of the liquid has evaporated.

5 Remove the pan from the heat and leave the sauce to cool slightly. Remove the bouquet garni and process the sauce, including the lemon rind, through a food mill, working in batches if necessary.

6 Adjust the seasoning, if necessary, being generous with freshly ground black pepper. If not using the sauce at once, cool, then cover and refrigerate for up to 3 days.

COOK'S TIP

This sauce will freeze for up to 4 weeks. Do not freeze for longer, or the garlic may give the sauce a "musty" taste.

Spinach & Herb Orzo

Serve this quick and easy, vibrant green pasta dish with any broiled meat or seafood. Orzo, shaped like long grains of barley, is popular in southern Italian and Greek cooking.

Serves 4

INGREDIENTS

1 tsp. salt
9 oz. dried orzo
7 oz. baby spinach leaves
5½ oz. arugula
1 oz. fresh flat-leaf parsley
 leaves

1 oz. fresh cilantro leaves
4 scallions
2 tbsp. extra-virgin olive oil
1 tbsp. garlic-flavored olive oil
pepper

TO SERVE:
radicchio or other lettuce leaves
2 oz. feta cheese, well drained and
 crumbled (optional)
lemon slices

1 Bring 2 pans of water to a boil, and put 12 ice cubes in a bowl of cold water. Add the salt and orzo to one of the pans, return to a boil and cook for 8–10 minutes, or according to package instructions, until the pasta is tender.

2 Meanwhile, remove the spinach stems if they are tough. Rinse the leaves in several changes of water to remove any dirt. Coarsely chop the arugula, parsley, cilantro, and green parts of the scallions.

3 Put the spinach, arugula, parsley, cilantro, and scallions in the other pan of boiling water and blanch for 15 seconds. Drain and transfer to the iced water to preserve the color.

4 When the spinach, herbs, and scallions are cool, squeeze out all the excess water. Transfer to a small food processor and process.

Add the olive oil and garlic-flavored oil and process again until well blended.

5 Drain the orzo well and stir in the spinach mixture. Toss well and adjust the seasoning.

6 Line a serving platter with radicchio leaves and pile the orzo on top. Sprinkle with feta cheese, if desired, and garnish with lemon slices. Serve hot or cool to room temperature.

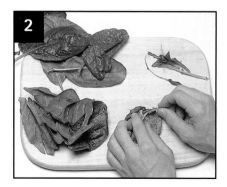

Spiced Pilau with Saffron

A Middle Eastern influence is evident in this fragrant pilau, studded with nuts, fruit and spices.
Serve with any roast lamb dish, or Spanish Chicken with Garlic (page 78).

Serves 4–6

INGREDIENTS

large pinch of good-quality saffron
   threads
2 cups water, boiling
1 tsp. salt
6 tbsp. butter
2 tbsp. olive oil

1 large onion, very finely chopped
3 tbsp. pine nuts
1 ¾ cups long-grain rice (not basmati)
½ cup golden raisins or raisins
6 green cardamom pods, shells lightly
   cracked

6 cloves
pepper
very finely chopped fresh cilantro or flat-
   leaf parsley, to garnish

1 Toast the saffron threads in a dry skillet over medium heat, stirring, for 2 minutes, or until they give off their aroma. Immediately pour them onto a plate.

2 Pour the boiling water into a measuring cup, stir in the saffron and 1 teaspoon salt, and set aside for at least 30 minutes to infuse.

3 Melt the butter with the oil in a skillet over medium-high heat. Add the onion and cook for about 5 minutes, stirring, until soft.

4 Lower the heat, stir in the pine nuts, and continue cooking for 2 minutes, stirring, until they just start to turn golden. Take care that they do not burn.

5 Stir in the rice, coating all the grains with oil. Stir for 1 minute, then add the golden raisins, cardamom pods, and cloves. Pour in the saffron-flavored water and bring to a boil.

Lower the heat, cover, and simmer for 15 minutes without removing the lid.

6 Remove from the heat and let stand for 5 minutes without uncovering. Remove the lid and check that the rice is tender, all the liquid has been absorbed, and the surface has small indentations all over.

7 Fluff up the rice. Adjust the seasoning, stir the herbs through, and serve.

Mediterranean Bread

Many of the flavors of the Mediterranean are captured in this rustic loaf.
It is perfect for sandwich making or for nibbling while enjoying a glass of wine.

Makes 1 loaf

INGREDIENTS

2³/₄ cups plus 2 tbsp. all-purpose flour, plus extra for sprinkling
1 envelope active dry yeast
1 tsp. salt

1 tbsp. coriander seeds, lightly crushed
2 tsp. dried oregano
³/₄ cup plus 2 tbsp. water, heated to 125°F on an instant-read thermometer
3 tbsp. olive oil, plus extra for greasing

5¹/₂ oz. sun-dried tomatoes in oil, drained, patted dry, and chopped
2³/₄ oz. feta cheese, drained, patted dry, and cubed
3¹/₂ oz. black olives, patted dry, pitted, and sliced

1 Stir the flour, yeast, salt, coriander seeds, and oregano together and make a well in the center. Slowly add most of the water and the olive oil to make a dough. Gradually add the remaining water, if needed, drawing in all the flour.

2 Turn out onto a lightly floured surface and knead for 10 minutes, gradually kneading in the sun-dried tomatoes, cheese, and olives. (The cheese will break up as

you knead.) Wash the bowl and lightly coat it with oil.

3 Shape the dough into a ball, put it in the bowl, and turn the dough over. Cover tightly and let the dough rise until it doubles in volume.

4 Turn the dough out onto a lightly floured surface. Knead lightly, then shape into a ball. Place on a lightly floured cookie sheet. Cover and let it rise until it doubles again.

5 Lightly sprinkle the top with flour. Using a sharp knife, cut 3 shallow diagonal slices in the top. Bake in an oven preheated to 450°F for 20 minutes. Lower the heat to 400°F and bake for 20 minutes longer, or until the loaf sounds hollow when you tap it on the bottom. Cool completely. This keeps well for up to 3 days in an airtight container.

Sesame Breadsticks

The irregular shape of these Greek-style breadsticks adds to their appeal.
They are crisp and crunchy on the outside with a soft, chewy interior.

Makes 32 sticks

INGREDIENTS

1³/₄ cups plus 2 tbsp. unbleached
  strong white flour
1³/₄ cups plus 2 tbsp. strong
  whole wheat flour
1 envelope active dry yeast

2 tsp. salt
¹/₂ tsp. sugar
2 cups water, heated to 125°F on an
  instant-read thermometer
4 tbsp. olive oil, plus extra for greasing

1 egg white, lightly beaten
sesame seeds, for sprinkling

1 Stir the flour, yeast, salt, and sugar together in a bowl and make a well in the center. Slowly stir in most of the water and the olive oil to make a dough. Gradually add the remaining water, if necessary, drawing in all the flour.

2 Turn out onto a lightly floured surface and knead for about 10 minutes until smooth. Wash the bowl and lightly coat with olive oil.

3 Shape the dough into a ball, put it in the bowl, and turn over so it is coated. Cover tightly with a dish towel and let the dough rise until it doubles in volume. Line a cookie sheet with waxed paper.

4 Turn out the dough onto a lightly floured surface and knead lightly. Divide the dough into 2 equal pieces. Roll each piece into a 16-inch rope and cut into 8 equal pieces. Cut each piece in half to make 32 pieces.

5 Cover the dough you are not working with as you roll each piece into a thin 10-inch rope, on a very lightly floured surface. Carefully put on the cookie sheet.

6 Cover and let rise for 10 minutes. Brush with the egg white, then sprinkle evenly and thickly with sesame seeds. Bake in a preheated oven at 450°F for 10 minutes.

7 Brush again with egg white, and bake for a further 5 minutes, or until golden brown and crisp. Cool on wire racks.

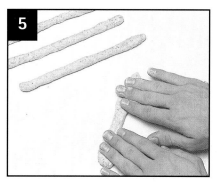

Olive Rolls

These country-style bread rolls depend on fruity olive oil and good-quality olives for their rich flavor. Use Greek kalamata olives, or any of the Flavored Olives (see page 172).

Makes 16 rolls

INGREDIENTS

4 oz. olives in brine or oil, drained
6¼ cups unbleached strong white
   flour, plus extra for dusting
1½ tsp. salt
1 envelope active dry yeast

2 cups water, heated to 125°F on an
   instant-read thermometer
2 tbsp. fruity extra-virgin olive oil,
   plus extra for brushing

4 tbsp. finely chopped fresh oregano,
   parsley, or thyme leaves, or 1 tbsp.
   dried mixed herbs

1 Pit the olives with an olive or cherry pitter and finely chop. Pat off the excess brine or oil with paper towels. Set aside.

2 Stir the flour, salt, and yeast together in a bowl and make a well in the center. Slowly stir in most of the water and the olive oil to make a dough. Gradually add the remaining water, if necessary, drawing in all the flour.

3 Lightly knead in the olives and herbs. Turn out onto a lightly floured surface and knead for 10 minutes. Wash the bowl and lightly coat with oil.

4 Shape the dough into a ball, put it in the bowl, and turn over so it is coated. Cover tightly with a dish towel and let it rest until it doubles in volume. Dust a cookie sheet with flour.

5 Turn out the dough onto a lightly floured surface and knead lightly. Roll the dough into 8-inch ropes on a very lightly floured surface.

6 Cut the dough into 16 even-sized pieces. Shape each one into a ball and place on the prepared cookie sheet. Cover and let rise for 15 minutes.

7 Lightly brush the top of each roll with olive oil. Bake in a preheated oven at 425° F for 25–30 minutes, or until the rolls are golden brown. Cool on a wire rack.

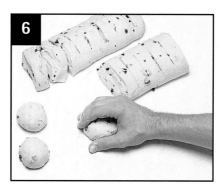

Fougasse

This distinctive-looking bread, with its herringbone slits, is baked daily throughout Provence. Like the traditional French baguette, it contains no fat, so it doesn't keep well and is best eaten on the day it is baked.

Makes 2 large loaves

INGREDIENTS

6 ¼ cups unbleached strong white flour, plus extra for kneading and dusting

1 envelope active dry yeast
2 tsp. salt
1 tsp. sugar

2 cups water, heated to 125°F on an instant-read thermometer
olive oil, for greasing

1 Stir the flour, yeast, salt, and sugar together in a bowl and make a well in the center. Slowly stir in most of the water to make a dough. Gradually add the remaining water, drawing in all the flour. If you need extra water, add it tablespoon by tablespoon.

2 Turn out onto a lightly floured surface and knead for 10 minutes until smooth. Wash the bowl and lightly coat with olive oil. Shape the dough into a ball, put it in the bowl and turn the dough over. Cover the bowl tightly with a dish towel and let rise until the dough doubles in volume.

3 Punch down the dough and turn out onto a lightly floured surface. Knead lightly, then cover with the upturned bowl and let rest for 10 minutes.

4 Put a roasting pan of water in the bottom of the oven while it preheats to 450°F. Lightly flour a cookie sheet.

5 Divide the dough into 2 pieces, and roll each one into a 12-inch oval, ½ inch thick. Using a sharp knife, cut five 3-inch slices on an angle in a herringbone pattern on each of the dough ovals. Cut all the way through the dough, using the tip of the knife to open the slits.

6 Spray the loaves with cold water. Bake for 20 minutes, turn upside down and continue baking for 5 minutes until the loaves sound hollow when tapped on the bottom. Cool on wire racks.

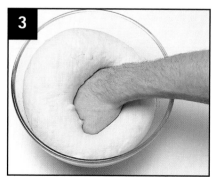

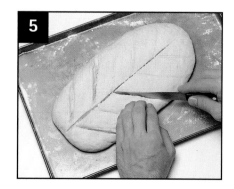

Herb Focaccia

Rich with olive oil, this bread is so delicious you can serve it on its own to accompany a glass of wine. For extra flavor, slice 2 oz. Flavored Olives (see page 172) and knead them into the dough.

Makes 1 loaf

INGREDIENTS

3⅓ cups unbleached strong white flour, plus extra for dusting
1 envelope active dry yeast
1½ tsp. salt

½ tsp. sugar
1¼ cups water, heated to 125°F on an instant-read thermometer

3 tbsp. good-quality fruity extra-virgin olive oil, plus extra for greasing
4 tbsp. finely chopped fresh herbs
polenta or cornmeal, for sprinkling
coarse sea salt, for sprinkling

1 Stir the flour, yeast, salt, and sugar together in a bowl and make a well in the center. Slowly stir in most of the water and 2 tablespoons of the olive oil to make a dough. Gradually add the remaining water, if necessary, drawing in all the flour.

2 Turn out onto a lightly floured surface and knead. Transfer to a bowl and lightly knead in the herbs for 10 minutes until soft but not sticky. Wash the bowl and lightly coat with olive oil.

3 Shape the dough into a ball, put it in the bowl, and turn the dough over. Cover tightly with a dish towel and let rise until the dough doubles in volume. Sprinkle polenta over a cookie sheet.

4 Turn the dough out onto a lightly floured surface and knead lightly. Cover with the upturned bowl and let stand for 10 minutes.

5 Roll and pat the dough into a 10-inch circle, about

½ inch thick, and place on the prepared cookie sheet. Cover with a dish towel and let rise for 15 minutes.

6 Using a lightly oiled finger, poke indentations all over the surface. Drizzle the remaining 1 tablespoon of olive oil over and sprinkle lightly with sea salt. Bake in a preheated oven at 450° F for 15 minutes, or until golden and the loaf sounds hollow on the bottom. Cool on a wire rack.

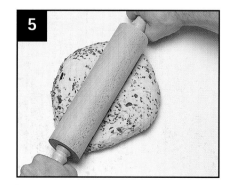

Sangria

Few images can be as evocative of a Spanish Mediterranean holiday as a pitcher of fruity Sangria. This punch is ideal to serve with a selection of Spanish tapas.

Makes 8–10 glasses

INGREDIENTS

1 large orange	½ cup sugar, or to taste	4-inch piece of cucumber
1 lemon	4 cups full-flavored Spanish wine,	ice cubes, to serve
2 peaches	such as Rioja	

1 Cut the orange into thin slices, then cut the slices into wedges. Place in a large ceramic or glass pitcher. Cut one long slice of rind from the lemon and add to the orange.

2 Slice completely around the peaches, cutting down to the pit. Twist the halves in opposite directions, until the 2 halves come apart. Remove and discard the pit. Slice the peach and add to the orange. Repeat with the remaining peach.

3 Add the sugar to the fruit and stir. Pour in the wine and stir until the sugar dissolves. Taste and add more sugar or a squeeze or two of lemon juice to taste. Chill for at least an hour.

4 Meanwhile, dice the piece of cucumber or cut it into stick shapes.

5 When ready to serve, use a long-handled wooden spoon to stir and press the fruit against the side of the pitcher to extract some of the juice. Put the ice cubes into glasses and pour the chilled sangria over. Add some fruit from the pitcher to each glass, then add the cucumber. Serve at once.

VARIATIONS

Red wine is traditional to use in this popular drink, but you can use white wine as well. For a party, add a drop of brandy before you chill the sangria. Limes can also be used in this drink.

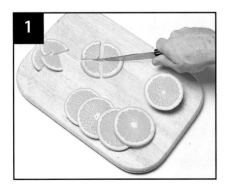

Desserts

Mediterranean fruit, like the region's vegetables, really benefit in terms of flavor from ripening under the intense sun. They are juicy and succulent, and a platter of simply prepared fruit can make the perfect end to a meal.

For simple recipes that don't adulterate the fruit's natural flavor, try ripe figs with a subtle orange-blossom cream, or Creamy Fruit Parfait, with peaches, apricots, and cherries, from the Greek island of Kythera, the birthplace of Aphrodite. Or, when strawberries are just past their peak, serve Balsamic Strawberries with Mascarpone—the unlikely combination of ground pepper and balsamic vinegar will highlight any flavor there is left.

However, not all Mediterranean desserts are fruit-based. The Middle Eastern influence on Turkish and Moroccan cooking means very sweet desserts are enjoyed with small cups of strong, dark espresso coffee. Few desserts can be sweeter than Baklava, thin layers of crisp filo pastry filled with spiced and sweetened chopped nuts and soaked in a sugar syrup. If you want something more comforting, there's a Creamy Rice Pudding from Greece, flavored with lemon.

The Italians are known for their excellent ice creams, so try the Lavender Ice Cream or Mint-chocolate Gelato. When you are in a hurry, few desserts can be quicker than Italian Drowned Ice Cream—hot espresso poured over homemade vanilla ice cream.

Balsamic Strawberries with Mascarpone

Generations of Italian cooks have known that the unlikely combination of freshly ground black pepper and ripe, juicy strawberries is fantastic. A splash of balsamic vinegar turns this simple dessert into a sensational dessert.

Serves 4–6

INGREDIENTS

1 lb. fresh strawberries
2–3 tbsp. best-quality balsamic
    vinegar

pepper
fresh mint leaves, torn, plus extra to
    decorate (optional)

4–6 oz. mascarpone cheese

1 Wipe the strawberries with a damp cloth, rather than rinsing them, so they do not become soggy. Using a paring knife, cut off the green stalks at the top and use the tip of the knife to remove the core.

2 Cut each strawberry in half lengthwise, or into quarters if large. Transfer to a bowl.

3 Add the vinegar, allowing ½ tablespoon per person. Add several twists of ground black pepper, then gently stir together. Cover with plastic wrap and chill for up to 4 hours.

4 Just before serving, stir in torn mint leaves to taste. Spoon the mascarpone cheese into individual bowls and spoon the berries on top. Decorate with a few mint leaves, if desired. Sprinkle with extra pepper to taste.

VARIATION

Replace the mascarpone cheese with Vanilla Ice Cream (see page 228), or a premium commercial vanilla or strawberry ice cream.

COOK'S TIP

This is most enjoyable when it is made with the best-quality balsamic vinegar, one that has aged slowly and has turned thick and syrupy. Unfortunately, the genuine mixture is always expensive. Less expensive versions are artificially sweetened and colored with caramel, or taste of harsh vinegar.

Figs with Orange-blossom Cream

Luscious, sweet fresh figs are piled high on market stalls throughout the Mediterranean during the summer, and feature on many restaurant menus. Here they are served with a delicate sauce, flavored with a hint of orange.

Serves 4

INGREDIENTS

8 large fresh figs
4 large fresh fig leaves, if available,
    rinsed and dried

CREME FRAICHE (OPTIONAL):
2 tbsp. buttermilk
1¼ cups heavy cream

ORANGE-BLOSSOM CREAM:
½ cup crème fraîche, homemade (see
    below) or bought
about 4 tbsp. orange-blossom water
1 tsp. orange-blossom honey
finely grated rind of ½ orange
2 tbsp. slivered almonds, to decorate
    (optional)

1 If you are making the crème fraîche, begin at least a day ahead. Put the buttermilk in a preserving jar or a jar with a screw top. Add the cream, securely close, and shake to blend. Allow to set at warm room temperature for 6–8 hours, then refrigerate for at least 8 hours and up to 4 days. It will develop a slight tangy flavor. Lightly beat before using.

2 To toast the almonds for the decoration, place in a dry skillet over medium heat and stir until lightly browned. Take care that they do not burn. Immediately pour the almonds out of the pan. Set aside.

3 To make the orange-blossom cream, put the crème fraîche in a small bowl and stir in 4 tablespoons of the orange-blossom water, with the honey and orange rind. Taste and add a little extra orange-blossom water if necessary.

4 To serve, cut the stems off the figs, but do not peel them.

Stand the figs upright with the pointed end upward. Cut each into quarters without cutting all the way through, so you can open them out into attractive "flowers."

5 If you are using fig leaves, place one in the center of each serving plate. Arrange 2 figs on top of each leaf, and spoon a small amount of the orange-flavored cream alongside them. Sprinkle the cream with the toasted slivered almonds if desired, just before serving.

Oranges in Spiced Caramel

The Moorish influence in southern Spain is evident in the use of spices in this easy, make-ahead dessert. This is particularly refreshing after a spicy meal.

Serves 4–6

INGREDIENTS

4 large, juicy oranges
4–6 tbsp. shelled pistachio nuts, chopped, to decorate

SPICED CARAMEL
1¼ cups superfine sugar
5 black peppercorns, lightly crushed

4 cloves
1 green cardamom pod, lightly crushed
1¼ cups water

1 To make the spiced caramel, put the sugar, peppercorns, cloves, cardamom pod, and ⅔ cup of the water in a pan and stir to dissolve the sugar over medium heat. When the sugar has dissolved, turn up the heat and boil, without stirring, until the syrup thickens and turns a deep caramel color. Use a wet pastry brush to brush down the side of the pan if necessary.

2 Very carefully, pour in another ⅔ cup water, standing back because it will splatter. Remove from the heat and, using a long-handled wooden spoon, stir until all the caramel has dissolved. Let cool.

3 Pare off the orange rind and pith, cutting carefully so the oranges retain their shape. Leave the oranges whole, or, working over a bowl, cut into segments, cutting the flesh away from the membranes.

4 Pour over the syrup with the spices and stir together. Cover and chill until ready to serve. Serve in individual bowls with chopped pistachio nuts sprinkled over the tops at the last minute.

VARIATION

Turn this Spanish dessert into a Sicilian-style one by using the blood-red oranges that grow in great profusion on the island.

Creamy Fruit Parfait

*On the tiny Greek island of Kythera, this luscious combination of
summer fruits and yogurt is served at tavernas as well as in homes.*

Serves 4–6

INGREDIENTS

8 oz. fresh, juicy cherries
2 large peaches
2 large apricots

3 cups Greek Strained Yogurt (see page 182), or natural thick yogurt
½ cup walnut halves

2 tbsp. flower-scented honey, or to taste
fresh red currants or berries, to decorate (optional)

1 To prepare the fruit, use a cherry or olive pitter to remove the cherry pits. Cut each cherry in half. Cut the peaches and apricots in half lengthwise and remove the stones (pits), then finely chop the flesh.

2 Place the finely chopped cherries, peaches, and apricots in a bowl and gently stir together.

3 Spoon one-third of the yogurt into an attractive glass serving bowl. Top with half the fruit mixture.

4 Repeat with another layer of yogurt and fruit, then top with the remaining yogurt.

5 Place the walnuts in a small food processor and pulse until chopped but not finely ground. Sprinkle the walnuts over the top layer of the yogurt.

6 Drizzle the honey over the nuts and yogurt. Cover the bowl with plastic wrap and chill for at least 1 hour. Decorate the bowl with a small bunch of red currants, if using, just before serving.

VARIATIONS

Vary the fruit to whatever is best in the market. Berries, figs, seedless grapes, and melons are also delicious in this simple family-style dessert. In winter, replace the fresh fruit salad with a dried fruit compote: cover dried fruit, such as apples, apricots, pitted dates, and figs, in orange juice until they plump, then proceed with the recipe.

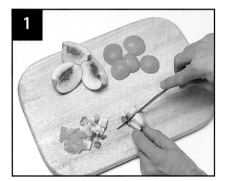

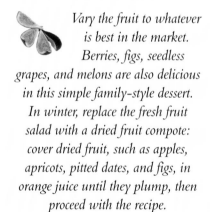

Poached Peaches with Amaretto-Mascarpone Cream

Soaking the peaches overnight is an old Turkish tip to prevent the fruit from becoming too soft and falling apart while they are being poached.

Serves 4–6

INGREDIENTS

8–12 ripe peaches
1 large lime
2 cups fruity, dry white wine
1 tbsp. black peppercorns, lightly crushed
3-inch cinnamon stick, halved

finely pared rind of 1 unwaxed lemon
1/2 cup superfine sugar
fresh mint sprigs, to decorate

AMARETTO-MASCARPONE CREAM:
2 tbsp. amaretto liqueur, or to taste
1 cup plus 2 tbsp. mascarpone cheese

1 Fill a large bowl with iced water. Bring a large pan of water to a boil. Add the peaches and cook for 1 minute. Using a slotted spoon, immediately transfer the peaches to the iced water to stop the cooking process.

2 Squeeze the juice from the lime into a bowl of water. Peel the peaches, then quarter each and remove the pit. Drop the fruit into the lime water as it is prepared. Cover and refrigerate for 24 hours.

3 Meanwhile, make the amaretto-mascarpone cream. Stir the amaretto into the mascarpone, cover and refrigerate.

4 Place the wine, peppercorns, cinnamon, lemon rind, and sugar in a saucepan over medium-high heat, and stir until the sugar dissolves.

5 Boil the syrup for 2 minutes. Reduce to a simmer. Remove the peaches, add them to the syrup, and poach for 2 minutes, or until tender—they should not be falling apart.

6 Using a slotted spoon, transfer the peaches to a bowl. Bring the syrup to a boil and continue boiling until thickened and reduced to about 1/2 cup. Pour the syrup into a heatproof bowl and cool. When cool, pour over the peaches. Cover and chill until required. To serve, decorate with mint.

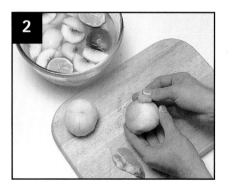

Creamy Rice Pudding with Lemon & Pistachio Nuts

Rice is a staple ingredient in many Mediterranean kitchens and here it is transformed into a creamy, family-style dessert. At the height of summer, serve well chilled with a mixture of summer berries.

Serves 4

INGREDIENTS

1 tsp. cornstarch
3¾ cups milk, plus an extra
   2 tbsp.

¾ cup short-grain rice
about 2 tbsp. sugar, or 1 tbsp. honey,
   to taste

finely grated rind of 1 large lemon
freshly squeezed lemon juice, to taste
½ cup shelled pistachio nuts

1 Place the cornstarch in a small bowl and stir in 2 tablespoons milk, stirring until no lumps remain. Rinse a pan with cold water and do not dry it out.

2 Place the remaining milk and the cornstarch mixture in the pan over medium-high heat, and heat, stirring occasionally, until it simmers and forms small bubbles all around the edge. Do not boil.

3 Stir in the rice, lower the heat, and continue stirring for 20 minutes, or until all but about 2 tablespoons of the excess liquid has evaporated and the rice grains are tender.

4 Remove from the heat and pour into a heatproof bowl. Stir in sugar to taste. Stir the lemon rind into the pudding. If a slightly tarter flavor is required, stir in freshly squeezed lemon juice. Allow to cool completely.

5 Tightly cover the top of the cool rice with a sheet of plastic wrap and chill in the refrigerator for at least one hour—the colder the rice is, the better it tastes with fresh fruit.

6 Meanwhile, using a sharp knife, finely chop the pistachio nuts. To serve, spoon the rice pudding into individual bowls and sprinkle with the chopped nuts.

COOK'S TIP

It is important to rinse the saucepan in Step 1 to prevent the milk from scorching on the sides or base of the pan.

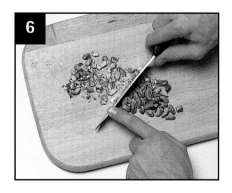

Spanish Flan

This classic dessert of baked custard with a caramel topping is delicious—much better than the commercially produced version found in restaurants along the Spanish Mediterranean! It is best made a day in advance.

Serves 4–6

INGREDIENTS

butter, for greasing	4 tbsp. water	1 vanilla bean
³/₄ cup plus 2 tbsp. superfine sugar	¹/₂ lemon	2 large eggs
	2¹/₄ cups milk	2 large egg yolks

1 Lightly grease the sides of a 5-cup souffle dish. To make the caramel, put a scant ⅓ cup sugar with the water in a pan over medium-high heat and cook, stirring, until the sugar dissolves. Boil until the syrup turns a deep golden brown.

2 Immediately remove from the heat and add a few drops lemon juice. Pour into the souffle dish and swirl around. Set aside.

3 Pour the milk into a pan. Slit the vanilla bean lengthwise and add it to the milk. Bring to a boil, remove the pan from the heat, and stir in the remaining sugar, stirring until it dissolves. Set aside.

4 Beat the eggs and egg yolks together in a bowl. Pour the milk mixture over them, whisking. Remove the vanilla bean. Strain the egg mixture into a bowl, then transfer to the souffle dish.

5 Place the dish in a roasting pan with enough boiling water to come two-thirds up the side.

6 Bake in a preheated oven at 325°F for 75–90 minutes until a knife inserted in the center comes out clean. Cool completely. Cover with plastic wrap and refrigerate for at least 24 hours.

7 Run a round-bladed knife around the edge. Place an up-turned serving plate with a rim on top, then invert the plate and dish, giving a sharp shake halfway over. Lift off the souffle dish and serve.

COOK'S TIP

The lemon juice is added to the caramel in Step 2 to stop the cooking process, to prevent it from burning.

Orange Crème à Catalanas

This creamy custard dessert, with its crisp, caramelized topping, is always popular in Spain.
it is not baked, it is much creamier than the similar-looking French crème brulée.

Serves 8

INGREDIENTS

4 cups milk	9 large egg yolks	3 tbsp. cornstarch
finely grated rind of 6 large oranges	1 cup superfine sugar, plus extra for the topping	

1 Put the milk and orange rind in a saucepan over medium-high heat. Bring to a boil, then remove from the heat, cover, and allow to cool for 2 hours.

2 Return the milk to the heat and simmer for 10 minutes. Put the egg yolks and sugar in a heatproof bowl that will sit over a saucepan with plenty of room underneath. Beat until creamy and the sugar dissolves.

3 Add 5 tablespoons of the flavored milk to the cornstarch, stirring until smooth. Stir into the milk. Strain the milk into the eggs, whisking until blended.

4 Rinse out the pan and put a layer of water in the bottom. Put the bowl on top of the pan, making sure the base does not touch the water. Simmer over medium heat, whisking, until the custard is thick enough to coat the back of a wooden spoon, which can take 20 minutes. Do not boil.

5 Pour into eight ⅔ cup ramekins and allow to cool. Cover each with a piece of plastic wrap and put in the refrigerator to chill for at least 6 hours.

6 When ready to serve, sprinkle the top of each ramekin with a layer of sugar. Use a kitchen blowtorch to melt and caramelize the sugar. Allow to stand for a few minutes until the caramel hardens, then serve at once. Do not return to the refrigerator or the topping will become soft.

COOK'S TIP

A kitchen blowtorch is the best way to melt the sugar quickly and guarantee a crisp topping. These are sold at good kitchen-supply stores, but if unavailable melt the sugar under a preheated hot broiler.

Italian Drowned Ice Cream

A classic vanilla ice cream is topped with steaming coffee to make a wonderful instant dessert.
Remember to serve in heatproof bowls.

Serves 4–6

INGREDIENTS

about 2 cups freshly made espresso
coffee
chocolate-covered coffee beans, to
decorate

VANILLA ICE CREAM:
1 vanilla bean
6 large egg yolks
$\frac{2}{3}$ cup superfine sugar, or Vanilla-
flavored sugar (see page 254)

2$\frac{1}{4}$ cups milk
1 cup plus 2 tbsp. heavy cream

1 To make the ice cream, slit the vanilla bean lengthwise and scrape out the tiny brown seeds. Set aside.

2 Put the yolks and sugar in a heatproof bowl that will sit over a saucepan with plenty of room underneath. Beat the eggs and sugar together until thick and creamy.

3 Put the milk, cream, and vanilla seeds in the pan over low heat and bring to a simmer. Pour the milk over the egg mixture, whisking. Place 1 inch water in the bottom of a pan.

Place the bowl on top, ensuring the base does not touch the water. Turn the heat to medium-high.

4 Cook the mixture, stirring constantly, until it is thick enough to coat the back of the spoon. Remove from the heat, transfer to a bowl, and allow to cool.

5 Churn the mixture in an ice-cream maker, following the manufacturer's instructions. Alternatively, place it in a freezerproof container and freeze for 1 hour. Turn out into a bowl

and whisk to break up the ice crystals, then return to the freezer. Repeat 4 times at 30-minute intervals.

6 Transfer the ice cream to a freezerpoof bowl, smooth the top and cover with plastic wrap or foil. Freeze for up to 3 months.

7 Soften in the refrigerator for 20 minutes before serving. Place scoops of ice cream in each bowl. Pour coffee over them and sprinkle with coffee beans.

Mint-chocolate Gelato

Rich, creamy gelati, or ice creams, are one of the great Italian culinary contributions to the world.
This one is made with fresh mint, which grows wild throughout the Mediterranean.

Serves 4–6

INGREDIENTS

6 large eggs
³/₄ cup superfine sugar
1¹/₄ cups milk

²/₃ cup heavy cream
large handful fresh mint leaves,
  rinsed and dried

2 drops green food coloring
  (optional)
2 oz. dark chocolate, finely chopped

1 Put the eggs and sugar in a heatproof bowl that will sit over a saucepan with plenty of room underneath. Using an electric mixer, beat the eggs and sugar together until thick and creamy.

2 Put the milk and cream in the saucepan and bring to a simmer, where small bubbles appear all around the edge, stirring. Pour onto the eggs, whisking constantly. Rinse the pan and put 1 inch water in the bottom. Place the bowl on top, making sure the base does not touch the water. Turn the heat to medium-high.

3 Transfer the mixture to a pan and cook the mixture, stirring constantly, until it is thick enough to coat the back of the spoon and leave a mark when you pull your finger across it.

4 Tear the mint leaves and stir them into the custard. Remove the custard from the heat. Cool, then cover and infuse for at least 2 hours, chilling for the last 30 minutes.

5 Strain the mixture through a small plastic strainer, to remove the pieces of mint. Stir in

the food coloring, if using. Churn in an ice-cream maker for 20 minutes, adding the chocolate pieces when the mixture becomes thick and almost frozen. If you don't have an ice-cream maker, freeze and whisk as in Step 5, Vanilla Ice Cream (see page 228).

6 Transfer to a freezerproof bowl, smooth the top and cover with plastic wrap or kitchen foil. Freeze for up to 3 months. Soften in the refrigerator for 20 minutes before serving.

Lavender Ice Cream

This rich and creamy dessert, with a hint of fresh lavender, captures the flavor of summer days in Provence when the purple-blue flowers scent the air. Be generous with the flowers because the freezing dulls their flavor.

Serves 6–8

INGREDIENTS

flowers from 10–12 large sprigs fresh lavender, plus extra to decorate
6 large egg yolks

¾ cup superfine sugar, or Lavender Sugar (see Cook's Tip)
2¼ cups milk

1 cup plus 2 tbsp. heavy cream
1 tsp. vanilla extract

1 Strip the small flowers from the stems, without any brown or green bits. Place them in a small strainer and rinse, then pat dry with paper towels. Set aside.

2 Put the eggs and sugar in a heatproof bowl that will sit over a saucepan with plenty of room underneath. Using an electric mixer, beat the eggs and sugar together until they are thick.

3 Put the milk, cream, and vanilla in the saucepan over low heat and bring to a simmer, stirring. Pour the hot milk over the egg mixture, whisking constantly. Rinse the pan and place 1 inch water in the bottom. Place the bowl on top, making sure the base does not touch the water. Turn the heat to medium-high.

4 Cook the mixture, stirring, until it is thick enough to coat the back of the spoon.

5 Remove the custard from the heat and stir in the flowers. Cool, then cover and set aside to infuse for 2 hours, chilling for the last 30 minutes. Strain the mixture through a

COOK'S TIP

To make Lavender Sugar, put 500 g/ 1lb. 2 oz. sugar in a food processor and add 125 g/4½ oz. lavender flowers, stripped from their stems. Process until blended, then leave in a sealed container for 10 days. Sift out flower bits and store the sugar in a sealed jar.

plastic strainer to remove the flowers.

6 Churn in an ice-cream maker, following the manufacturer's instructions. Alternatively, freeze and whisk as in Step 5, Vanilla Ice Cream (see page 228).

7 Transfer to a freezerproof bowl, smooth the top and cover with plastic wrap or kitchen foil. Freeze for up to 3 months. Soften in the refrigerator for 20 minutes before serving. Decorate with lavender flowers.

Orange & Bitters Sorbet

Made from a distinctive Italian drink and freshly squeezed orange juice,
this smooth, pale-pink sorbet is a cooling dessert with a refreshing tang.

Serves 4–6

INGREDIENTS

3–4 large oranges
1 cup plus 2 tbsp. superfine
   sugar

2½ cups water
3 tbsp. red Italian bitters, such as
   Campari

2 large egg whites
fresh mint leaves and Candied Citrus
   Peel (see page 178), to decorate
   (optional)

1 Working over a bowl to catch any juice, pare the rind from 3 of the oranges, without removing the bitter white pith. If some of the pith does come off with the rind, use the knife to scrape it off.

2 In a saucepan, dissolve the sugar in the water over low heat, stirring. Increase the heat and boil for 2 minutes without stirring. Using a wet pastry brush, brush down the side of the pan, if necessary.

3 Remove the pan from the heat and pour into a heatproof non-metallic bowl. Add the orange rind and let it infuse while the mixture cools to room temperature.

4 Roll the pared oranges back and forth on the work surface, pressing down firmly. Cut them in half and squeeze ½ cup juice. If you need more juice, squeeze the extra orange.

5 When the syrup is cool, stir in the orange juice and bitters. Strain into a container, cover, and chill for at least 30 minutes.

6 Put the mixture in an ice-cream maker and churn for 15 minutes. Alternatively, follow the instructions on page 228. Whisk the egg whites in a clean bowl until stiff.

7 Add the egg whites to the ice-cream maker and continue churning for 5 minutes, or according to the manufacturer's instructions. Transfer to a shallow, freezerproof container, cover, and freeze for up to 2 months.

8 About 15 minutes before serving, soften in refrigerator. Scoop into bowls and serve, decorated with mint leaves and the Candied Citrus Peel, if wished.

Lemon Granita

*Soft and granular, this iced dessert has a sharp, zingy flavor
that is refreshing and ideal for rounding off any rich meal.*

Serves 4–6

INGREDIENTS

4 large unwaxed lemons

½ cup superfine sugar
3 cups water

mint sprigs (optional) to decorate

1 Pare 6 strips of rind from one lemon, then finely grate the remaining rind from the remaining lemons, being very careful not to remove any bitter white pith.

2 Roll the lemons back and forth on the work surface, pressing down firmly. Cut each in half and squeeze ½ cup juice. Add the grated rind to the juice. Set aside.

3 Put the pared strips of lemon rind, sugar, and water in a saucepan and stir over low heat to dissolve the sugar. Increase the heat and boil for 4 minutes, without stirring. Use a wet pastry brush to brush down any spatters on the side of the pan. Remove from the heat, pour into a non-metallic bowl, and cool.

4 Remove the strips of rind from the syrup. Stir in the grated rind and juice. Transfer to a shallow metal container, cover, and freeze for up to 3 months.

5 Chill serving bowls 30 minutes before serving. To serve, invert the container onto a chopping board. Rinse a cloth in very hot water, wring it out, then rub on the bottom of the container for 15 seconds. Give the container a shake and the mixture should fall out. If not, repeat.

6 Use a knife to break up the granita and transfer to a food processor. Quickly process until it becomes granular. Serve at once in the chilled bowls (or in scooped-out lemons). Decorate with mint sprigs, if desired.

VARIATION

Lemon-scented fresh herbs add a unique and unexpected flavor. Add 4 small sprigs lemon balm or 2 sprigs lemon thyme to the syrup in Step 3. Remove and discard with the pared rind in Step 4. Or stir ½ tablespoon finely chopped lemon thyme into the mixture in Step 4.

Espresso Granita

Enjoy this crunchy granita as a cooling mid-morning snack or as a light dessert.
It is great with Lavender Hearts (see page 250).

Serves 4–6

INGREDIENTS

1 cup superfine sugar
2¹/₂ cups water
¹/₂ tsp. vanilla extract

2¹/₂ cups very strong espresso coffee,
chilled

fresh mint, to garnish

1 Put the sugar in a saucepan with the water and stir over low heat to dissolve the sugar. Increase the heat and boil for 4 minutes, without stirring. Use a wet pastry brush to brush down any spatters on the side of the pan.

2 Remove the pan from the heat and pour the syrup into a heat-proof non-metallic bowl. Set the bowl in the kitchen sink filled with iced water to speed up the cooling process. Stir in the vanilla and coffee and let cool completely.

3 Transfer to a shallow metal container, cover, and freeze for up to 3 months.

4 Thirty minutes before serving, place serving bowls in the refrigerator to chill.

5 To serve, invert the container onto a chopping board. Rinse a cloth in very hot water, wring it out, then rub on the bottom of the container for 15 seconds. Give the container a sharp shake and the mixture should fall out. If not, repeat.

6 Use a knife to break up the granita and transfer to a food processor. Quickly process until it becomes grainy and crunchy. Serve at once in the chilled bowls, decorated with mint.

COOK'S TIP

A very dark, fruit-flavored espresso is the only choice for this Italian specialty. Otherwise the flavor will be marred by the freezing.

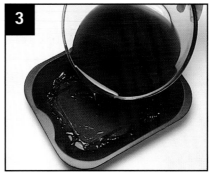

Italian Ricotta-lemon Cheesecake

Italian bakers pride themselves on their baked ricotta cheesecakes, studded with fruit soaked in spirits, and you will find them adorning the windows of the best pasticcerias all along the Italian Mediterranean.

Serves 6–8

INGREDIENTS

1³/₄ oz. golden raisins
3 tbsp. marsala or grappa
butter, for greasing
semolina, for dusting
1¹/₂ cups ricotta cheese, drained
3 large egg yolks, beaten
¹/₂ cup superfine sugar

2 tbsp. semolina
3 tbsp. lemon juice
2 tbsp. candied orange peel,
   homemade (see page 178) or store
   bought, finely chopped
finely grated rind of 2 large lemons

TO DECORATE:
confectioners' sugar
mint sprigs
fresh red currants or berries
   (optional)

1 Soak the golden raisins in the marsala or grappa in a small bowl for about 30 minutes, or until the spirit has been absorbed and the fruit is swollen.

2 Meanwhile, cut out a circle of waxed paper to fit the base of a 8-inch round cake pan with a removable base that is about 2 inches deep. Grease the side and base of the pan and line the base. Lightly dust with semolina and shake out the excess.

3 Using a wooden spoon, press the ricotta cheese though a plastic strainer into a bowl. Beat in the egg yolks, sugar, semolina, and lemon juice, beating until blended.

4 Fold in the golden raisins, orange peel, and lemon rind. Pour into the prepared pan and smooth the surface.

5 Bake the cheesecake in the center of a preheated oven at 350° F for 30–40 minutes until firm when you press the top, and slightly coming away from the side of the pan.

6 Turn off the oven and open the door. Allow the cheesecake to cool in the turned-off oven for 2–3 hours. To serve, remove from the pan and transfer to a plate. Sift a layer of confectioners' sugar over from at least 12 inches above the cheesecake to lightly dust the top and sides. Decorate with mint and red currants, if desired.

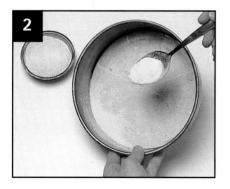

Tarte au Citron

*Few desserts can be more appealing to round off a meal
on a hot evening than this creamy, tangy tart.*

Serves 6–8

INGREDIENTS

grated rind of 2–3 large lemons
$^2/_3$ cup lemon juice
$^1/_2$ cup superfine sugar
$^1/_2$ cup heavy cream or crème fraîche
3 large eggs

3 large egg yolks
confectioners' sugar, for dusting

CRUST:
1$^1/_4$ cups all-purpose flour
$^1/_2$ tsp. salt
8 tbsp. cold unsalted butter, diced

1 egg yolk beaten with 2 tbsp.
ice-cold water

1 To make the crust, sift the flour and salt into a bowl. Using your fingertips, rub the butter into the flour until the mixture resembles fine crumbs. Add the egg yolk and water and stir to make a dough.

2 Gather the dough into a ball, wrap in plastic wrap, and refrigerate for at least 1 hour. Roll out on a lightly floured work surface and use to line a 9–10 inch fluted tart pan with a removable base. Prick the base all over with a fork and line with a sheet of waxed paper and baking beans.

3 Bake in a preheated oven at 400°F for 15 minutes until the pastry looks set. Remove the paper and beans. Reduce the oven temperature to 375°F.

4 Beat the lemon rind, lemon juice, and sugar together until blended. Slowly beat in the cream or crème fraîche, then beat in the eggs and yolks, one by one.

5 Set the pastry case on a cookie sheet and pour in the filling. Transfer to the preheated oven and bake for 20 minutes until the filling is set.

6 Cool completely on a wire rack. Dust with confectioners' sugar. Serve with Candied Citrus Peel (see page 178).

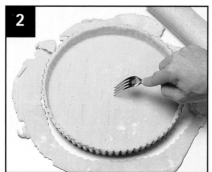

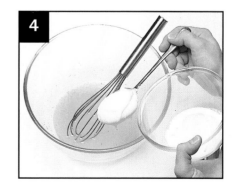

Chocolate Pine Nut Tartlets

Rich and creamy-textured pine nuts and orange rind are popular ingredients in both sweet and savory Mediterranean dishes—here they add a twist of flavor to luscious chocolate tartlets.

Makes 8 tartlets

INGREDIENTS

2 oz. dark chocolate with at least 70% cocoa solids
4 tbsp. unsalted butter
³/₄ cup plus 2 tbsp. superfine sugar
5 tbsp. light brown sugar
6 tbsp. milk
3¹/₂ tbsp. light corn syrup

finely grated rind of 2 large oranges and 2 tbsp. freshly squeezed juice
1 tsp. vanilla extract
3 large eggs, lightly beaten
3¹/₂ oz. pine nuts

CRUST:
1³/₄ cups all-purpose flour
pinch of salt
7 tbsp. butter
1 cup confectioners' sugar
1 large egg and 2 large egg yolks

1 To make the pastry, sift the flour and a pinch of salt into a bowl. Make a well in the center and add the butter, confectioners' sugar, whole egg, and egg yolks. Using your fingertips, mix the ingredients in the well into a paste.

2 Gradually incorporate the surrounding flour to make a soft dough. Quickly and lightly knead the dough. Shape into a ball, wrap in plastic wrap, and chill for at least 1 hour.

3 Roll the pastry into eight 6-inch circles. Use to line eight 4 inch tartlet pans with removable bases. Line each with waxed paper to fit, and top with baking beans. Chill for 10 minutes.

4 Bake in a preheated oven at 400°F for 5 minutes. Remove the paper and beans and bake for a further 8 minutes. Cool on a wire rack. Reduce the oven temperature to 350°F.

5 Meanwhile, break the chocolate into a saucepan over medium heat. Add the butter and stir until blended.

6 Stir in the remaining ingredients. Spoon the filling into the tartlet cases on a cookie sheet. Bake for 25–30 minutes, or until the tops puff up and crack and feel set. Cover with waxed paper for the final 5 minutes if the pastry is browning too much. Transfer to a wire rack and allow to cool for at least 15 minutes before removing from pan. Serve warm or at room temperature.

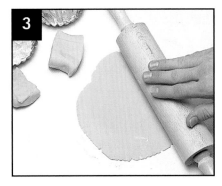

Baklava

Incredibly sweet, baklava can almost be considered the national dessert of Greece and Turkey. Once home cooks made their own wafer-thin filo pastry, but now it is easy to buy.

Makes 25 pieces

INGREDIENTS

2 cups walnut halves
1¾ cups shelled pistachio nuts
¾ cup blanched almonds
4 tbsp. pine nuts, finely chopped
finely grated rind of 2 large oranges
6 tbsp. sesame seeds
1 tbsp. sugar
½ tsp. ground cinnamon

½ tsp. ground allspice
about 1¼ cups butter, melted
23 sheets filo pastry, each 10 inches
  square, defrosted if frozen

SYRUP:
3 cups superfine sugar
2¼ cups water
5 tbsp. honey
3 cloves
2 large strips lemon rind

1 To make the filling, put the walnuts, pistachio nuts, almonds, and pine nuts in a food processor and pulse until finely chopped but not ground. Transfer to a bowl and stir in the orange rind, sesame seeds, sugar, cinnamon, and allspice.

2 Butter a 10-inch square ovenproof dish that is 2 inches deep. Cut the stacked sheets to size, using a ruler. Keep the sheets covered with a damp dish towel.

3 Place a sheet of filo on the bottom of the dish and brush with melted butter. Top with 7 more sheets, brushing with butter between each layer.

4 Sprinkle with a generous 1 cup of the filling. Top with 3 more sheets of filo, brushing each one with butter. Continue layering until all the filo and filling are used, ending with a top layer of 3 sheets of filo. Brush with butter.

5 Using a very sharp knife and a ruler, cut into twenty-five 2-inch squares. Brush again with butter. Bake in a preheated oven at 325°F for 1 hour.

6 Meanwhile, put all the syrup ingredients in a saucepan, stirring to dissolve the sugar. Bring to a boil, then simmer for 15 minutes, without stirring, until a thin syrup forms. Cool.

7 Remove the baklava from the oven and pour the syrup over the top. Allow to set in the dish, then remove the squares to serve.

Cannoli

No Sicilian wedding or celebration is complete without these delicate rolls. If you can't find the molds, use large dried pasta tubes, covered with kitchen foil, shiny side out.

Makes about 20 rolls

INGREDIENTS

3 tbsp. lemon juice
3 tbsp. water
1 large egg
1³/₄ cups all-purpose flour
1 tbsp. superfine sugar
1 tsp. ground allspice
pinch of salt

2 tbsp. butter, softened
sunflower oil, for deep-frying
1 small egg white, lightly beaten
confectioners' sugar

FILLING:
3¹/₄ cups ricotta cheese, drained
4 tbsp. confectioners' sugar

1 tsp. vanilla extract
finely grated rind of 1 large orange
4 tbsp. very finely chopped candied
   fruit
1³/₄ oz. dark chocolate, grated
pinch of ground cinnamon
2 tbsp. marsala or orange juice

1 Combine the lemon juice, water, and egg. Put the flour, sugar, spice, and salt in a food processor and quickly process. Add the butter, then, with the motor running, pour the egg mixture through the feed tube. Process until the mixture just forms a dough.

2 Turn the dough out onto a lightly floured surface and knead lightly. Wrap and chill for at least 1 hour.

3 Meanwhile, make the filling. Beat the ricotta cheese until smooth. Sift in the confectioners' sugar, then beat in the remaining ingredients. Cover and chill until required.

4 Roll out the dough on a floured surface until ¹/₁₆ inch thick. Using a ruler, cut out 3 ½ x 3 inch pieces, re-rolling and cutting the trimmings; you should make about 20 pieces.

5 Heat 2 inches oil in a pan to 375°F. Roll a piece of pastry around a greased cannoli mold, barely overlapping the edges. Seal the edges with egg white, pressing firmly. Repeat with all the molds you have. Fry 2 or 3 molds until golden, crisp, and bubbly.

6 Remove with a slotted spoon and drain on paper towels. Leave until cool, then carefully slide off the molds. Repeat with the remaining pastry.

7 Store unfilled in an airtight container for up to 2 days. Pipe in the filling no more than 30 minutes before serving to prevent the pastry from becoming soggy. Sift confectioners' sugar over and serve.

Lavender Hearts

*"Seas" of lavender cover the Provence countryside during the summer,
and not surprisingly, local bakers incorporate the distinctive flavor into many sweet recipes.*

Makes about 48 cookies

INGREDIENTS

$1^2/_3$ cups all-purpose flour, plus extra
   for dusting
7 tbsp. chilled butter, diced
6 tbsp. Lavender Sugar (see page 232),
   or ordinary superfine sugar

1 large egg
1 tbsp. dried lavender flowers, very
   finely chopped

TO DECORATE:
about 4 tbsp. confectioners' sugar
about 1 tsp. water
about 2 tbsp. fresh lavender flowers

1 Line 2 cookie sheets with waxed paper. Put the flour in a bowl, add the butter, and lightly rub in with your fingertips until the mixture resembles fine crumbs. Stir in the sugar.

2 Lightly beat the egg, then add to the flour and butter mixture with the lavender flowers. Stir to form a stiff paste.

3 Turn out the dough onto a lightly floured work surface and roll out until about ¼ inch thick.

4 Using a 2-inch heart-shaped cookie cutter, press out 48 cookies, occasionally dipping the cutter into extra flour, and re-rolling the trimmings as necessary. Transfer the pastry hearts to the cookie sheets.

5 Prick the surface of each heart with a fork. Bake in a preheated oven at 350°F and bake for approximately 10 minutes, or until the cookies are lightly browned. Transfer to a wire rack set over a sheet of waxed paper to cool.

6 Sift the confectioners' sugar into a bowl. Add 1 teaspoon cold water and stir until a thin, smooth icing forms, adding a little extra water if necessary.

7 Drizzle the icing from the tip of the spoon over the cooled cookies in a random pattern. Immediately sprinkle with the fresh lavender flowers while the icing is still soft so that they stick in place. Leave for at least 15 minutes until the icing has set. Store for up to 4 days in an airtight container.

Almond Cookies

Almond trees grow in abundance all over the Mediterranean region, so the slightly sweet nut is another frequent ingredient in both savory and sweet recipes.

Makes about 32 cookies

INGREDIENTS

generous 1 cup unblanched almonds
1 cup butter, softened

6 tbsp. confectioners' sugar, plus
   extra for sifting
scant 2 cups all-purpose) flour

2 tsp. vanilla extract
1/2 tsp. almond extract

1 Line 2 cookie sheets with waxed paper. Using a cook's knife, finely chop the almonds, or process them in a small food processor, taking care not to overprocess them into a paste. Set aside.

2 Put the butter in a bowl and beat with an electric mixer until smooth. Sift in the confectioners' sugar and continue beating until creamed and smooth.

3 Sift in the flour from above the bowl and beat it in until blended. Add the vanilla and almond extracts and beat again to form a soft dough. Stir in the chopped almonds.

4 Using a teaspoon, shape the dough into 32 round balls about the size of walnuts. Place on the prepared cookie sheets, spacing them apart. Bake in a preheated oven at 350°F for 20–25 minutes until set and just starting to turn brown.

5 Let the cookies stand on the cookie sheets for 2 minutes to firm up. Sift a thick layer of confectioners' sugar over them. Transfer to a wire rack and let cool completely.

6 Lightly dust with more confectioners' sugar, just before serving. Store in an airtight container for up to one week.

VARIATION

Although not a true Mediterranean ingredient, pecans can be used instead of the almonds. Add 2 teaspoons finely grated orange rind to the dough in Step 3.

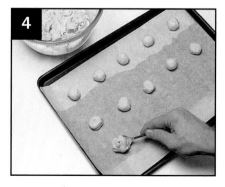

Vanilla Tea Cake with Glacé Candied Fruit

Slices of juicy fruit slowly soaked in sugar syrup are one of the great delicacies of Provence and southern Italy. They make a glorious flavoring for this cake.

Makes 12–15 slices

INGREDIENTS

8 oz. quality candied fruit, such as cherries and orange, lemon, and lime peels, or Candied Citrus Peel (see page 178)
³/₄ cup ground almonds
finely grated rind of ¹/₂ lemon

generous ¹/₂ cup all-purpose flour
generous ¹/₂ cup self-rising flour
³/₄ cup butter, softened, plus extra for greasing
³/₄ cup plus 2 tbsp. vanilla-flavored sugar (see Cook's Tip)

¹/₂ tsp. vanilla extract
3 large eggs, lightly beaten
pinch of salt
candied fruit, to decorate

1 Grease a 8¹/₂ x 4¹/₂ x 2-inch bread pan with butter, then line the base with a piece of waxed paper.

2 Chop the fruit into small uniform pieces, reserving a few of the larger slices for the top. Place in a bowl with the ground almonds, lemon rind, and 2 tablespoons of the measured flour, and stir together. Set aside.

3 Beat the butter and sugar together until fluffy and creamy. Beat in the vanilla extract and eggs, a little at a time.

4 Sift both flours and the salt into the creamed mixture, then fold in. Fold in the fruit and ground almonds.

5 Spoon into the pan and smooth the surface. Arrange the reserved fruit on the top.

Loosely cover the pan with kitchen foil, making sure it does not touch the cake mixture. Bake in a preheated oven at 350°F for about 1¹/₂ hours until risen and a skewer inserted into the center comes out clean.

6 Cool in the pan on a wire rack for 5 minutes, then turn out and remove lining. Cool completely on a wire rack. Wrap in kitchen foil and store in an airtight container for up to 4 days. Serve decorated with candied fruit.

COOK'S TIP

Make your own vanilla-flavored sugar by storing a sliced vanilla bean in a closed jar of superfine sugar.

Index